PERCEPTION
and
Aesthetic Value

PERCEPTION

and

Aesthetic Value

by

HAROLD NEWTON LEE

Associate Professor of Philosophy
Newcomb College, Tulane University

NEW YORK
PRENTICE-HALL, INC.
1938

Reprinted with the permission of Prentice-Hall, Inc.

JOHNSON REPRINT CORPORATION
111 Fifth Avenue, New York, N.Y. 10003

JOHNSON REPRINT COMPANY LTD.
Berkeley Square House, London, W. 1

First reprinting, 1967, Johnson Reprint Corporation

Printed in the United States of America

Preface

A ESTHETICS is the study of the experience of a certain kind of value. In recent times, many important conclusions have been achieved in the theory of value, but, in spite of these, little in the field of aesthetics has been written to take advantage of them. The present work, by building a theory of aesthetics around the central concept of the nature of aesthetic value, attempts to correct this condition. A consideration of the aesthetic attitude, of the data of perception, and of the place of pleasure in the aesthetic experience leads to a definition of aesthetic value. The problems arising from the more complex aspects of the aesthetic experience, such as the problems of expression, taste, art, and criticism, are analyzed, and solutions are offered from the standpoint of the definition of aesthetic value.

Aesthetics is more than an analysis of beauty. It is more than a study of the principles of appreciation of either beauty or the fine arts. It is more than the study of the activity of artistic creation. Aesthetics is a philosophic science of fundamental importance. It investigates the nature of aesthetic value and displays the relation between this kind of value and other kinds.

Aesthetic value is the most characteristic example of intrinsic value. A rigorous study of aesthetic value goes to the heart of the problem of value as nothing else does. In addition, aesthetics deals with simple directness with the sources of all of our perceptual experience. Both epistemology and theory of value can learn much from aesthetics. Until philosophy in America realizes this and gives to aesthetics the fundamental emphasis it merits, the teaching of philosophy will remain, at least in this degree, inadequate.

Furthermore, art criticism (including music and literature, of course), art appreciation, and art education have much to learn from aesthetics. Most of our art criticism is haphazard. Much of our art education (again including music and literature) is so misdirected that it results only in stifling, more or less effectively, what native appreciation and native ability the children have. Both of these conditions could be rectified, or at least bettered, if critics and educators were versed in a fundamental knowledge of aesthetics.

The present volume grew from a thesis offered to the Department of Philosophy at Harvard University in 1930 in partial fulfillment of the requirements for the Ph. D. degree. It appeared to me at that time that the method of approach to the problems of aesthetics from the standpoint of the theory of value (or axiology, as it is coming to be called) should be explored. I found the approach both interesting and promising of fruitful conclusions. I hope the promise has been borne out. The material of the study was completely worked over and rewritten in 1933. This resulted in further clarification and systematization, and in the relegation of some of the material to appendices, where it does not intrude on the orderly development of the theory. A further revision was made in 1937.

My thanks are due to Mrs. Adele Robinson and Mrs. Helen Werthessen of the Art Department of Wellesley College, who read the manuscript in its early stages and helped me a great deal by their discussion of it and by direct suggestions. I also wish to thank Will H. Stevens of the Art School of Newcomb College, and Rudd Fleming of the Department of English, and Richard R. Kirk of the Department of English of Tulane University, and George T. Kalif of the Department of Psychology for reading the manuscript in its entirety and for making many helpful suggestions. My obligations to my former teachers and to students in classes in aesthetics are too numerous to mention, but to one former student, Miss Betty Cutting, I owe especial thanks for help in preparing the manuscript.

I am under great obligations to the editorial department of Prentice-Hall, Inc. for many helpful suggestions and for the pleasing appearance of the book.

H. N. LEE

Table of Contents

CHAPTER I

Introduction

1.

The aesthetic experience. The appreciation of beauty is an everyday experience for most men, but it is little understood even by those to whom it occurs most frequently. The lack of understanding, however, does not preclude the recognition of its unique character, for almost everyone realizes in a vague and indistinct way that the aesthetic experience is different from other kinds of experience. Without reflection, most persons can use such words as "beautiful," "pretty," "elegant," or "neat" with a fair degree of consistency and intelligibility. These words characterize the objects of the aesthetic experience and are not wholly appropriate to any other objects. Hence, by the use of them, one is implicitly recognizing an experience which is more or less unique. It is the first task of aesthetics clearly to understand the nature of this experience and to make definite the ordinary vague recognition of it.

This task is not easy, for even one who would affirm without hesitation that he experiences beauty now and then might find it peculiarly difficult to describe his experience with precision. This difficulty besets the study of aesthetics at the very outset: it is hard to give a satisfactory preliminary definition of the subject. Where such a preliminary definition is called for, it is customary to say either that aesthetics is the philosophy of beauty or that it is the philosophy of art. Neither of these definitions is very precise. They are by no means synonymous, yet both are intended to denote the same general field. To say that it is both the philosophy of beauty and the philosophy of art would be to deny beauty to anything but art, and also to affirm that all art is beautiful; and neither of these judgments could go unchallenged. To choose either of the definitions to the exclusion of the other would be to leave out of the general field a great deal that many inquirers consider essential.

In choosing between these two definitions, one would probably find less objection to the opinion that aesthetics is the philosophy of beauty, for certainly, the appreciation of beauty is a characteristic example of the aesthetic experience. This definition, however, creates two difficulties: there may be other aesthetic experiences in addition to the appreciation of beauty; and the word "beauty" is highly ambiguous. It is shot through and through with literary and poetic connotations such that it cannot be used with precision. And the opposite of beauty, ugliness, is not irrelevant. Attempts have been made to circumvent this objection by defining aesthetics as the philosophy of beauty and ugliness, but this manifestly is a make-shift.

`` The highest degree of beauty is probably to be found in art, and this would seem to give a basis for the view that aesthetics is the philosophy of art. `` Such a view is open to the objection that aesthetics is not a study of only the highest degree of the aesthetic experience. Furthermore, what art is is not at all clear. Is it an activity of the human spirit, or is it the name of the class of those objects which are artifacts? Is the subject of aesthetics all art, or only one division, known as "fine art," or more equivocally yet, as "aesthetic art"?

As it is impossible to settle these and similar questions in an offhand manner, it is better to start the study of aesthetics not from a preliminary definition but from the investigation of the aesthetic experience that everyone vaguely recognizes now and then. The experience of beauty may be taken as a characteristic example of this aesthetic experience. That those who have never given a moment's thought to the matter can use the term "beautiful" with a tolerable degree of satisfaction is sufficient warrant for taking this as a point of departure.

2.

Examples of the aesthetic experience. The care and attention which have been devoted, even from prehistoric times, to the ornamentation of tools and the surroundings of ordinary life bear witness that the aesthetic experience has played a large part in the life of man. Great effort always has been and is now expended merely on making things attractive to the eye. One puts a picture on the wall. Why? It does not make the room more comfortable. It in no way ministers to the economic necessities of life. It may have no sentimental value. It may be there only because the owner likes its appearance. He may think that it is beautiful, or that it adds to the scheme of interior decoration and makes the room more beautiful. This, roughly, is an example of the experience from which the study of aesthetics starts and which it seeks to understand.

One goes to an orchestral concert and sits enraptured, delighted simply to listen to the sounds that are being produced. He takes great pleasure in hearing them just because they sound the way they do. They have no intellectual significance. They may be an economic waste. Morally their import is doubtful. Yet the auditor listens to them and enjoys them. He exhibits a bodily condition which denotes great interest. He is undergoing the aesthetic experience.

The difference between this experience and the intellectual, the moral, and the practical would be admitted even by unreflective persons as soon as they were led to think about it. They would agree at once that one understands an algebraic proof in a way very different from that in which he appreciates the beauty of a sunset. Although a picture be morally evil, it yet might be beautiful. To condemn a piece of literature on moral or philistine grounds is not to say that it may not be fine writing. The kind of pleasure attendant upon the appreciation of a symphony is quite distinct from that attendant upon the news that a business venture has succeeded and produced a large profit.

Some persons seem to undergo the aesthetic experience more often than do others, and to a more intense degree. One often sees that the object by which he is moved is noted by another without a trace of interest. Sometimes he sees that another is experiencing delight in the presence of an object that leaves him cold and indifferent. And if he talks to others concerning their experiences, he finds that there are wide divergences of opinion. He finds some to whom questions of beauty are uppermost, many to whom such questions are of casual interest, and some who seem seldom to be aware of beauty or ugliness in their surroundings. If all this leads him to reflect, and to seek to understand the experiences of his neighbors and himself, then he has begun to be a philosopher and has undertaken the investigation called aesthetics.

3.

Aesthetics and the experience of value. The aesthetic experience is the experience of a certain kind of value. There are many different kinds of value: moral value, economic value, practical value, religious value, political value, intellectual value, and others. Among these various kinds is aesthetic value, one of the common names of which is beauty. It is a philosophic task to inquire into the nature of this value. What are the general characteristics of value? What distinguishes aesthetic value from other kinds? What are the relations between it and the others? What are the conditions for experiencing this kind of value?

Philosophy in general is an attempt rationally to understand experience and those things which experience seems to indicate to us. Hence, aesthetics is a branch of philosophy, as it is the attempt to understand one particular portion of experience and the nature of the value apprehended in that experience. The artist, the critic, and the psychologist can contribute valuable data concerning certain aspects of this experience and the processes to be understood. But the philosophical task lies in eliciting the general principles inherent in all the particular data and in systematically organizing them into coherent theory.

Of course, this task is intellectual. All philosophy arises from reflection and the attempt to reach understanding, and reflection and understanding are intellectual and cognitive. Hence, the study of aesthetics is intellectual and cognitive, but this in nowise indicates that the aesthetic experience is intellectual or cognitive. Aesthetics is the intellectual study of the experience of aesthetic value. This experience is not intellectual. Value is immediately apprehended; it is not understood as the result of a reasoning process. Reasoning processes may in some way influence its apprehension; this might be expected, as there is some sort of unity running through all experience. The apprehension of value is not created by the reasoning processes, however, even where it may be indirectly influenced by them; and these processes are not essential to it.

Value is immediately apprehended; hence the experience of value is more akin to the affective experience than to the intellectual. Value is felt, not known. The aesthetic experience is feeling, not knowledge. So apparent is this that many writers have treated the experience in terms of "the aesthetic emotion," even though they are most insistent that this emotion is quite different from "the common emotions of life." Whether or not the apprehension of value is emotional depends upon what the emotions are and what part they play in experience; therefore it cannot be stated without further investigation that the apprehension of aesthetic value is essentially an emotion. This is one of the psychological problems in aesthetics, and will be considered in due time. One of the reasons, however, why it is so easy to think of the aesthetic experience as an emotion is that it is not intellectual. The intellectual experience is mediated by reasoning processes and by concepts. The apprehension of value is not mediated, and in this is similar to the affective experience.

The aesthetic experience is not a kind of knowledge, but it is possible to have knowledge about it. The apprehension of aesthetic value is not a judgment, but it is possible to make judgments concerning it. When the mind reflects on its experiences of value, it makes judgments concerning them. When it compares one value with another, it makes judgments, and deals with the values in terms of the judgments concerning them. Any direct experience of value can be thus evaluated. An evaluation of an object is a *judgment* concerning the value of that object. The apprehension of value is a valuation, but a judgment concerning this valuation is an evaluation. Evaluations arise from the cognition of an actual situation; for example, of such a situation as the direct apprehension of value or the comparison of one value with another. Evaluations imply knowledge concerning one's previous apprehensions of value; that is, of his previous valuings.

Evaluations are, of course, intellectual and cognitive, for they are embodied in judgments. This in no way makes the value intellectual or cognitive. The evaluation is dependent upon the value. The value is fundamental; and its own nature is not affected by whatever may be done to it. It is evident that a thing must have value; that is, must be apprehended as valuable before any judgments concerning its value can be made.

Aesthetics, where it may be concerned with evaluations, is concerned with them only because they are about actual values. It may be true that immediate experiences are recorded in judgments and must be so recorded before aesthetics can deal adequately with them; but it does not follow from this that the subject matter of the study of aesthetics is a judgment. The aesthetic experience is the subject matter, and this is prior to any judgments that might be made concerning it. Aesthetic judgment is about aesthetic value, and the only reason that aesthetics is concerned with it is that it is about aesthetic value.

It is very important clearly to keep this in mind, because the problem of the relation of cognition to the aesthetic experience is a difficult one, and if an adequate solution is to be reached, there must be no confusion at the beginning of the investigation. The study is intellectual, but the subject matter of the study is an experience which is not intellectual or cognitive. In the more complex developments of the aesthetic experience, it may be found that cognitive factors at times have some sort of influence upon the apprehension of value, but this does not make the apprehension fundamentally a cognitive matter. If such influence is apparent in the more complex experiences, its consideration should be postponed until after the simpler elements of the experience have been ascertained, and it should be disregarded until that time. [1]

4.

The purpose of aesthetics. Of course, it is not necessary to understand all about value, valuing, and evaluating before one experiences aesthetic value. As has been emphasized already, the experience, in the nature of the case, has to come first, as it is the data for the understanding. To one who has not already experienced beauty, no possible definition of beauty can have significance; and likewise, unless one is acquainted with aesthetic value, the study of aesthetics will be meaningless. There is no reason to expect the study of aesthetics to stimulate appreciation, but there is no reason to expect it to inhibit it. It is not the function of the study either to stimulate or to inhibit, but merely to understand and to explain. Some persons will doubtless find that an increased understanding and clarification calls their attention to values that they would not have noted otherwise, and to these persons the study of aesthetics will be an aid to appreciation. Others may find that the understanding and explanation affects them as a dissection of what was an intimately living and unified experience. Where the study of aesthetics adversely affects one's appreciation, the study might well be abandoned, for it is probably more desirable to appreciate beauty than to understand it.

---

[1] This and other considerations of method which will be assumed in the text are more fully elaborated and defended in Appendix A, "Metaphysics and Aesthetics."

In any case, the way in which one's study affects his appreciation is his own personal idiosyncrasy. No necessary connection between the study of aesthetics and the encouragement or inhibition of appreciation can be established, but in another direction the study will usually show an effect. If one inquires into the nature of aesthetic value and the difference between it and other kinds of value, his ability to discriminate between the several kinds will be increased. He may find evidence to show that some of the signs he took to be signs of the aesthetic experience are really very confused, and indicate the experience of other kinds of value instead. In other words, as his judgment grows more critical, he may, and probably will, have reason slightly to modify and restrict the denotation of the terms "beautiful," "artistic," and so forth. He might find reason to question the uncritical assurance of his first impression that he or his neighbor was really having an aesthetic experience.

For example, one goes into one of the motion-picture theaters that a few years ago were built on a grand scale—"an acre of seats in a palace of splendor." He finds it teeming with elaborate display. The walls fairly crawl with gilt ornament, and one hardly feels himself touch the floor, so deep and soft are the carpets. He finds statuettes of polar bears on illuminated glass ice cakes, plaster casts of noted works of sculpture, and copies of famous paintings. To provide all this required an immense expenditure of money and effort, but it was done because it was assumed that people would enjoy looking at it. Perhaps they do enjoy looking at it, but possibly they have this enjoyment not because of its beauty, but because it is an immense display of wealth which is theirs vicariously for two hours at the price of thirty-five cents.

One goes into a room upon the wall of which is hanging a large and vivid chromolithograph of the battle of Bunker Hill, or of the victory of the *Robert E. Lee* over the *Natchez*, or of two or three bananas peeping coyly from the midst of a gigantic and luscious bunch of grapes. The person who lives in the room may like to look at the chromolithograph. In the study of aesthetics, the fact that he does so must not be disregarded; it may be an example of the experience that is being investigated. A case cannot be decided by throwing some of the relevant evidence out of court. At the outset, all the evidence that may possibly be relevant must be admitted. Only as the case proceeds may the evidence be sifted. But it also must not be assumed that because the owner likes to look at the picture it is good to look at. His sensitiveness to aesthetic value may be undeveloped: his appreciation may be undiscriminating. Perhaps he likes the *Battle of Bunker Hill* because a thrill of sentimentalized patriotism sweeps over him when he looks at it. The *Victory of the Robert E. Lee* may recall all he has read about the romantic old steamboat days on the Mississippi. The bananas may make his mouth water; but mouth watering is not beauty.

At the conclusion of the study of aesthetics, all these different reactions should be clearly understood, and the relations between them should be apparent. The aesthetic experience should be recognized not vaguely and indistinctly, but should be understood clearly and definitely. It is the aesthetic experience, an experience of a certain kind of value, which is being investigated, and although a critical survey may lead one to modify his first impressions, the modification must be always in the direction of a more complete clarification and understanding. It can never lead away from the experience with which it starts.

Any theory of aesthetics that lays down *a priori* rules of appreciation and decides what ought to be found beautiful even if it is not, and what ought not to be found beautiful even if it is, is to be distrusted for this reason. It has led away from the very experience it is supposed to be investigating. It is bad theory, because theory is the systematization of the principles that can be elicited from our actual experience. As far as both the creation of works of art and the appreciation of them go, such an aesthetics is so much rubbish, because the history of art has shown a tendency to lead toward "what should not be done," and finally to thrive on it. As philosophy, such a theory is worse than rubbish, because it brings the study of philosophy only into disrepute by engendering a false notion of its task and nature.

The actual experience, wherever it may be found, and whatever it may be, is the subject matter of aesthetics, and is what the philosophic study seeks rationally to comprehend and to understand. This experience is at first recognized in a vague and indefinite manner. Aesthetics takes this vague and indefinite material, critically investigates it, elicits theoretic principles from the evidence it can find, from whatever source it may come, and endeavors to work all these principles into a coherent and systematic theory which affords a basis for understanding and explaining aesthetic value in its most complex manifestations.

CHAPTER II

The Aesthetic Attitude

1.

The importance of the attitude and the object. It has been noted that the aesthetic experience is the apprehension of a certain kind of value. This value must be definitely and clearly distinguished from moral, practical, intellectual, and other kinds of value. Value arises in a certain relation between an individual and his environment. It does not have ontological subsistence of its own without reference to an apprehending individual. R. B. Perry has called this relation "interest," [1] but the term "interest" must be taken in a very fundamental, generic sense. Because it is not usually understood in such a broad sense, other writers have used the term "desire." But "desire" also bears too narrow a meaning. The concept of the

---

[1] R. B. Perry, *General Theory of Value,* New York, 1926.

relation giving rise to value is a generalization of all narrower modes of conation. This relation arises from the fact that the individual seeks or avoids contact with particular parts of his environment, and it finds its expression in an attitude of the individual. Any particular value, then, is a function of an attitude.

An attitude is always directed toward some object in the environment. The object is also a variable in the determination of the value. Hence any value is a function of two variables: the attitude or interest of the individual, and the environmental object of this attitude. The attitude and object are essential to each other: the relation between them is an internal relation, and it is in this relation that value becomes realized. Thus the terms of the relation are the conditions of value. Any kind of value can be defined by means of these two conditions, which are necessary and sufficient to it. A particular kind of attitude directed toward a particular kind of object gives rise to the apprehension of moral value. Another kind of attitude directed toward another kind of object gives rise to intellectual value, and so on. The kind of interest in the kind of object which gives rise to aesthetic value must be determined before a definition of that value can be reached. The aesthetic attitude and the nature of the object both must be ascertained. It is a lack of clarity on this point which has engendered the endless and futile disputes concerning the nature of beauty: whether it is subjective or objective.

2.

Example of the aesthetic attitude. The aesthetic attitude
will be considered first, and an example will aid in bringing out
its essential characteristics. Suppose that four laborers are
working in a field at sunset on a summer day. A distant
bell begins to ring, and one of them stops to listen to the
sound. He hears the tones. Attending only to their sound,
he is interested in them as they are in their own nature. If
the mere hearing of them gives him pleasure, they are beautiful to him. A second laborer, as soon as he hears the bell,
gathers up his tools and goes off in the direction of the village.
He takes the sounds to indicate that it is time to stop work
and go get his dinner. A third man, being a devout believer,
kneels down and prays. The bell is the Angelus, and calls
him to worship. The fourth man is a stranger to the region,
and, thinking that the bell may be a fire bell, he hastens off
to help those in distress.

The first man takes the aesthetic attitude. He is apprehending aesthetic value. The attitudes of the other three are
quite different from his. That of the second may be called
practical; that of the third, religious; and that of the fourth,
perhaps moral. It does not matter what the other three attitudes are called as long as it is noted that they all are *different
from the first in a characteristic way*: the attention of the first
man is wholly directed to the sound of the bell, but for the
other three the actual sounds are only signs of something else.

It matters no whit to the first whether the bell means dinner or prayer or fire. It may mean any or all, but apart from what it means, it is beautiful.

The actual physical stimulus is the same in all four cases. The same sounds from the same bell are carried through the same air and fall upon the ears of men in similar surroundings. And yet the reactions of the men do not have a great deal in common. Whence comes the difference? The only answer that psychology has to offer is that the mental attitude of each man is different. Each regards the actual stimulus in a different way—is interested in it for different reasons—and the resultant reaction is caused by this attitude toward the stimulus. The sounds call forth a response that is relative to the interest.

The responses of the last three men are actional in a way that the response of the first man is not. When they hear the bell, they do something about it. Of course, the response of the first man may be said to be actional too. His response involves an act of the attention; but the action here is very different from that of the other three. They become engaged in bodily activities, or at least, even if the ordinary response is inhibited, their attention is directed toward bodily activities in a manner from which the first man is wholly free. This is the reason why the aesthetic attitude often has been called *contemplative*.

The perception of the sounds is taken by the last three men to mean something in a sense in which it can be said to mean nothing at all to the first man. He is not interested in any significance that the sounds may have beyond their own intrinsic nature. He is pleased, not by what they indicate, but by how they sound. He is not interested in their causes or in their effects. This is the reason why the aesthetic attitude often has been called disinterested. It is not interested in the consequences of the immediate experience or in anything ulterior to it. In fact, the anticipation of consequences does not even exist for the aesthetic attitude. Only the perceptual appearance before it exists. One who takes this attitude is absorbed in the object as it appears immediately to perception.

3.

Another example of the attitude. This attitude has been described in other ways also. Bullough shows that when an object is regarded aesthetically it is given "psychical distance":

> The transformation of distance is produced in the first instance by putting the phenomenon, so to speak, out of gear with our practical actual self, . . . by looking at it "objectively," . . . and by interpreting even our subjective affections not as modes of *our* being but rather as characteristics of the phenomenon.[2]

H. S. Langfeld comments on this view of Bullough's, and his comment offers a splendid example of the aesthetic attitude:

> Let it be supposed that an individual is on a ship during a storm, and there is serious danger of a shipwreck. It is quite possible that even in such a situation, a man of artistic temperament would admire the movements of the waves, and the dash of the spray, entirely oblivious of danger, and with no concern as to what the high seas may ultimately do to the ship. Descriptions of such a state of mind, even in

---

[2] E. Bullough, "Psychical Distance." *British Journal of Psychology*, Vol. 5, p. 89.

situations of extreme danger, are frequently found in literature. For Dr. Bullough there would here be complete psychical distance. Suddenly, however, a wave larger than any previous one approaches and the artist's muscles set in preparation to meet the blow. Dr. Bullough would say that at that moment he has entirely lost his distance, that is, his aesthetic attitude. It will now be better understood why Dr. Bullough has termed the distance "psychical" for it denotes the mental attitude. In one instant the man is entirely lost in the shape of the wave and its force, and in the color of the water; in the next, although he still sees the shape and its color, he is interested only in his preparation to meet the contingency.[3]

These examples suffice to show the difference between the aesthetic attitude and the moral and practical attitudes. The moral and practical attitudes are interested in results which may follow the perception in point of time. The aesthetic attitude is not. It is interested in the perception only as it is immediately apprehended. It is interested in the perception for its own sake.

4.

The aesthetic attitude defined. The aesthetic attitude may be distinguished from the intellectual attitude, for the latter shows interest in the perceptual data only as signs or symbols that have meaning. It is concerned with the grasp of abstract or conceptual relations, such as the relations of implication, subsumption, equivalence, and so forth. The aesthetic attitude

---

[3] H. S. Langfeld, *The Aesthetic Attitude,* p. 57. New York. Harcourt, Brace and Co., 1920.—By permission of the publishers.

is not. It is concerned with the apprehension of the perceptual data. The intellectual attitude looks through or beyond these data at something which they signify. The aesthetic attitude is interested in appearance only, and by "appearance" is here meant not that which is rationally understood, but that which is perceptually apprehended. The aesthetic attitude is the attitude of complete occupation with perceptual data considered in their own nature, not as signifying or resulting in anything else. The aesthetic attitude is interest in perceptual data for their own sake.

In perception there is an appearance before the mind. This appearance may have been caused by something, it may mean something, it may involve something else, it may result in something else; but the aesthetic attitude is not concerned with any of these things. It is interested only in the perceptual appearance as it appears—as it is in its own nature. This does not imply that the mind is wholly passive in the aesthetic attitude. The notion that perception implies a purely passive and receptive state of mind was abandoned long ago. To determine exactly what the mind contributes to the percept is beyond the scope of aesthetics; but that it is active and contributive in perception is no longer subject to doubt.

The aesthetic attitude is concerned with the appearance that is before it, but this appearance is not totally independent of the mind.[4] There is a "creative element" in the aesthetic experience: it is the contribution which the mind makes in per-

---

[4] I do not mean to enter into metaphysical controversies here. What I have said is psychological, and may be interpreted according to the theories of any metaphysical school in the way that is advocated in Appendix A.

ception (and in the perceptual imagination). To say that the
aesthetic attitude is absorption in the perceptual aspects of experience does not exclude a contribution of the mind and
imagination in the apprehension of aesthetic value.

5.

Plan of further study. Value is the result of a unique relation between an individual and his environment. In the case
of aesthetic value, one term of this relation is the aesthetic attitude. Attention has to be paid to that which is given in perceptual intuition for its own sake, in its own nature, before
there can be any experience of aesthetic value (positive or negative). The value is apprehended only as a result of this attitude; but it is not created by the attitude alone, for an object
in the environment is also one of the terms of the relation from
which the value emerges.

The attitude is a necessary condition of the value, but is not
in itself sufficient. A further investigation must show the
nature of the object of this attitude. Even when this is found,
only a foundation has been laid for the complete understanding
of aesthetic value. Actual values are compared, and evaluations
are made. Some values seem more intense than others, and
the complete definition of aesthetic value must contain in it
some reference to an evaluating factor by means of which these
comparisons are made and this datum of intensity is explained.
The aesthetic attitude and the nature of the object that elicits
and satisfies this attitude are the sufficient conditions for aesthetic
value. The evaluating factor is what determines the degree of

intensity of this value; more of this factor makes it more intense, and less makes it less intense.

Of the following chapters, III and IV will investigate the object of the aesthetic experience. Chapter V will deal with the evaluating factor. Chapter VI will define aesthetic value. Chapters VII and VIII will treat of problems which enter into the complex manifestations of the experience; and the last three chapters will show the application of this theory of aesthetics to the analysis of art and of other matters that occur in the ordinary course of experience and with which aesthetics must deal.

CHAPTER III

Perception

1.

The materials of the aesthetic experience. The aesthetic attitude has been defined as attention directed toward perceptual data considered in their own nature and for their own sake; it is complete occupation with these data, or an interest manifested wholly in them. This definition indicates that all the materials of the aesthetic experience are perceptual in character. The nature of the object of the aesthetic experience is that it is a perceptual object. This characterization, however, is very general, and itself needs further elucidation.

In terms of concrete denotation, just what are the materials of beauty? If a sunset is beautiful, what are the materials of which this beauty is composed? In the case of the sunset, the answer is rather easy: they are the colors and cloud patterns. The beauty is aesthetic value, and the object which is beautiful, that is, the object of the aesthetic experience, is the perceived colors, shapes, and lines. The materials from which the beauties of painting and sculpture are constructed are also colors, shapes, lines, and textures. Sounds, the harmonies and movements of tones, are the materials of music. These are all perceptual in an obvious way: they are apprehended through the senses.

The question might be asked, however, what are the materials of poetry? Are they simple perceptions in the same sense as are the colors and patterns of a sunset? Poetry is made of words, but are words only spoken sounds? If the beauty of poetry is to be found only in the sound of the words, poetry is a species of music, and is nothing more. Most persons agree that literary art is more than music; hence, although the sound of the words is an important element in the beauty of poetry, there are other materials. Are these the shapes and colors of the letters which spell the words? One rarely takes an asthetic attitude toward them in appreciating poetry: they are more or less extraneous. Are they the images suggested by the meanings of the words? These images are objects of the aesthetic attitude, and are essential to the beauties of poetry. They are perceptual, but not in the' same obvious sense as is the case of the colors of a sunset.

W. T. Stace, in *The Meaning of Beauty,* calls attention to the fact that in ordinary discourse we may refer to the beauty of some men's characters.[1] Perhaps this is a figure of speech:

---

[1] W. T. Stace, *The Meaning of Beauty,* London, 1929, pp. 14-18.

perhaps we mean by it that the character is morally good in an unusual sort of way. In case it has literal meaning, however, the character must be envisaged in terms of perceptual materials toward which an aesthetic attitude can be taken. It may be possible to find such materials. There are many persons who think of moral characters in terms of dramatic imagery that is perceptual, and these persons can call a character beautiful with some degree of literalness. Here again, however, the aesthetic materials are not perceptual in exactly the same way as are the colors of a sunset.

The determination of the fundamental nature of the object of the aesthetic experience necessitates a clear understanding and careful definition of perception. The last two examples have shown clearly that perception is not to be identified with sensation, for they refer to aesthetic experiences whose materials are not unequivocally sensuous.

2.

Perception distinguished from sensation. The materials of beauty are not only sensuous, for perception is not to be confused with sensation. The term "sensation" has been carefully defined by psychology, and if one uses it as defined, it is not always correct to say that the object of the aesthetic experience is given in sensation. The term "sensation" means the conscious response to the stimulation of a sense organ, or nerve receptor. In adult life, at least, this response is seldom the whole content of consciousness. Together with the sensations is given their organization: structural and qualitative relations are data as well as the simple sensations themselves. The whole datum usually present to consciousness is not a sensation but a perception. In present-day psychology, sensations are conceived rather abstractly to be the content of perceptions, and are known only as a result of analysis, by abstraction from perceptions.

Perception involves selection among sensations, combination, organization, and sometimes supplementation from the imagination.[2]   Perception takes place in the light of the past experience of the organism, and consequently there may be factors in it for which no actually direct physical stimulus is present. There are psychological and physiological determinants in perception, as well as stimulus determinants. From the point of view of the source, sense images are to be distinguished from sensations, yet both may be the content of perception. The sense images may involve highly elaborate co-ordinations of one sense with another, as when the eye sees distance although the actual visual sensory field is flat. One has no visual *sensation* of distance *per se,* but one does *perceive* a third dimension in the field of vision.

Sensation is amorphous; perception is of form. This form may be due to a more adequate grasp of the putative metaphysical cause of the sensation; or it may be something *a priori* which is added by the synthetic activity of a mind; or it may be due to the dynamic stresses in the physiological processes of the

---

[2] I do not mean to imply by this that perceptions are constructed by a synthetic activity of the mind working with separately given sensations.   I am merely using the language of analysis for purposes of explanation.

brain. The determination of the cause of the fact that perception is of form has little bearing on the problems of aesthetics. No matter what the metaphysical or psychological theory of the cause of the difference between perception and sensation may be, yet the difference is present, and that is all that need be noted by aesthetics. The bare sensory nature of any object is not that toward which the aesthetic attitude is directed. The attitude is directed toward that which is given in perception.

3.

The distinction between sensation and perception solves the problem of "the aesthetic senses." The importance of the discrimination between sensation and perception can be illustrated by a problem that has often puzzled those who reflect on their aesthetic experiences. Is one speaking literally or in a metaphor when he calls an odor or a taste beautiful? Does an epicure experience aesthetic value when he eats of a finely concocted salad or a well-seasoned cheese? Is it not using language loosely and without precision to call even the bouquet of fine wine or the odor of a rose beautiful?

Ever since Plato and Aristotle, it has been maintained by some that sight and hearing are the aesthetic senses: sensations of sight and hearing can be beautiful, but the stimulation of the "lower senses" cannot. This view has a specious plausibility, but it is fundamentally in error in assuming that any sensations, as sensations, are aesthetic. The material of the aesthetic experience is perception. The plausibility arises from the fact that most perceptions are built around sight and hearing; therefore the material of most aesthetic experiences is made up largely of sights and sounds.

The "objective world" is principally given through sight and hearing; consequently perception, with its "objective reference," is usually based on the activities of these two senses. The stimulations of the other senses enter into perception mainly as they are added to or interpreted in the light of sight and hearing. By themselves they tend to be amorphous, since the organs are not developed to the degree of discrimination of the eye and the ear, and to remain more nearly on the level of sensations. Most persons live in a world of sight and sound. The bulk of their perceptions are based on the eye and the ear. An equally large proportion of their aesthetic experiences will seem to contain mostly sight and hearing as content.[3]

Originally, the view that these senses are the aesthetic senses can be traced to Plato's moralism. He thought of sight as akin to the way the soul knows the Ideas. Hearing seems to be in the same class as sight because it ministers to divine discourse. The "lower senses," he thought, are merely appetitive and must be subordinated. Aside from the questionable support which this view of Plato's gives, any attempt to maintain that aesthetic experiences must in the nature of the case be visual or auditory and that the "lower senses" cannot furnish the materials of beauty seems to be based on sheer dogmatism.

---

[3] The specious plausibility of the view that sight and hearing are the aesthetic senses is further increased by the fact that developed art techniques are either visual or auditory. D. W. Prall, in *Aesthetic Judgment* (New York, 1929), has well pointed out that these techniques are structures built upon the intrinsic orders of sensuous material, and clear intrinsic orders seem to inhere only in visual and auditory material. See especially Chapter V.

The object of the aesthetic attitude is that which can be perceived (or perceptually imagined). Sensations are the content of perceptions, and hence there seems to be no reason to talk about the aesthetic and the nonaesthetic senses. The only sensuous experience which could not be aesthetic would be one which did not become the content of perception and hence could not be the object of the aesthetic attitude. There may be sensuous experiences of this kind, such as sexual gratification, or an intense pain, or a sudden, very loud noise. It is doubtful that such experiences can be called perceptual. It is true that most perceptions are based on sight and hearing, and that therefore most aesthetic experiences are concerned with content that comes primarily through the eye and the ear; but this in no way makes the "lower senses" nonaesthetic. If tastes, smells, or sensations of touch enter into perceptual complexes toward which an aesthetic attitude is taken, then they are materials of beauty. In so far as an aesthetic attitude is taken toward the odor of the rose, then the odor is a beautiful object.

4.

Perceptual intuition distinguished from perception of fact. The term "perception" is ambiguous unless it is pointed out exactly in what sense it is to be used. There are two moments of perceptual experience, or rather, two kinds of perception: perception of fact (*Wahrnehmung*); and pure perception, or perceptual intuition (*Anschauung*).[4] Perception of fact is cognitive and intellectual. It involves the activity of the understanding. In the language of Kant, perception of fact subsumes the data of intuition under a concept. Perceptual intuitions (*Anschauungen*) are present in perceptions of fact, but they are regarded merely as symbols. In ordinary experience, one is interested in perceptions only in so far as they have significance to action or to understanding: only as they can be interpreted as signs of facts. He really pays little attention to the percepts in their own nature, for his interest lies elsewhere. He looks past the percept at something ulterior.

All this is saying that when one is perceiving facts he is not in the aesthetic attitude. Therefore, the perception of fact (if it can correctly be called perception), as it is not the object of the aesthetic attitude, is not the material of the aesthetic experience. It does not fit within the description of the aesthetic attitude because it is not concerned with the percepts only as they are in their own nature—that is, only as percepts. Although the perception of fact as such is not aesthetic, there is something aesthetic contained within it, for the intuited data are present even if they are not attended to but are regarded only as signs. A house, a tree, a cat, a mill whistle, a piece of ice—these are all facts. But colored shapes, felt shapes with

---

[4] I do not use the term "pure perception" in the way Kant uses it (*reine Anschauung*) in the first few pages of the Transcendental Aesthetic in the *Critique of Pure Reason*. By "pure perception" Kant means that which is free from the empirical. I mean that which is free from the intellectual. I am not convinced that there is any meaning whatever in speaking of perception or intuition which is free from the empirical.

their textures and temperatures, sounds and tones—these are all perceptual intuitions.

One often says, "I hear a street car." In all strictness, does one hear a street car? A street car can hardly be defined as a sort of a noise, but it is the noise that one hears. It is hardly strictly accurate even to say "I see a street car," because a street car is more than a colored shape. A street car is both of these and in addition is what one can do with it and what it can do to one. Of course, we shall all continue to say that we hear and see street cars, and quite correctly, for in this phrase the hearing and seeing refers to perception of fact, not strictly to perceptual intuition. The datum which is immediately before consciousness is the noise or the colored shape. This is perceptual intuition, but by means of it we make the judgment of fact that there is a street car. The perceptual intuitions are what is given to consciousness, and it is by means of them that one makes judgments of fact, but when one is making the judgment of fact he is not regarding the data in their own nature and for their own sake.

Only perceptual intuition is aesthetic. This intuition is the awareness of the perceptual data. Anything beyond is extraneous. Perception of fact uses this intuited data as signs and symbols, but this is beyond intuition. Perceptual intuition is not "synthetic," nor it is discursive. If it were either, it could not be called intuition. Perceptual intuition is the direct awareness of that organization of data immediately apprehended through the senses or in sense imagery. The term "perception" is used in the present study to signify perceptual intuition unless specific attention is called to some different use of it. The term "aesthetic" to mean "perceptual" (in this and only this sense) goes back to the derivation of the word from αἴσθεσις, which is usually translated "sense perception."

The distinction between perceptual intuition and perception of fact will be seen later to have an important bearing on the problem of representation in the arts.[5] When one judges painting or sculpture according to the fidelity of its representation, he is concerned primarily with facts, not with intuitions, and hence is not in the aesthetic attitude. This does not mean, however, that representation is irrelevant to painting, for even when one is attending to the intuitions, it may nevertheless be true that the intuitions are organized into facts.

5.

The distinction between sensation, perceptual intuition, and perception of fact is analytical. In concrete experience, it may be that sensations, perceptual intuitions, and perceptions of fact are never found separate from each other. Sensations are content for perceptual intuitions,[6] which in turn may be content for perceptions of fact. The distinction between these three is analytical, but there is no difficulty in keeping it clear even though the three factors cannot be exhibited separately. Nor is there any reason for blurring the general distinction because it might appear difficult to draw a precise dividing line between perceptual intuition and sensation on the one hand, and be-

---

[5] These questions will be more fully discussed in Chapter IX, Section 9.

[6] Sense images may also be content for perceptual intuition.

tween perceptual intuition and the perception of fact on the other. The theoretic dividing line is made by the definitions themselves and has the same degree of precision. The distinction is made in practice by the aesthetc attitude. The attitude has been defined as complete occupation with perceptual data considered in their own nature; and when one considers the data *in their own nature,* that means they are the data of perceptual intuition.

It is unnecessary to exhibit in concrete experience a precise dividing line because, as was pointed out above, sensation is rarely the whole content of consciousness in adult experience. Where a pure sensation might be conceived to be the whole content of consciousness, it cannot be called a perception. The sensation is amorphous, and there is in its nature no structure, no organization, no clear definition. There is no object of sensation, but perception is always objectively directed. Even if the sensation of intense pain or of sexual gratification is the whole *content* of consciousness, it is not the *object* of consciousness. Even the simplest percept, such as a colored shape or a single tone, is an *object* of consciousness. Furthermore, even the simplest percept has form. An adult never hears merely a tone: he hears a high tone or a low tone, a loud tone or a gentle tone, a harsh tone or a mellow tone. He never sees merely color: he sees red with all its given relations to purple and orange, or orange with all its given relations to red and yellow. He sees a color in its relation to the circle of hues and the scales of intensity and saturation.[7] All this is aside from

---

[7] The excellent treatment of the intrinsic orders of the materials of hearing and vision in Prall's *Aesthetic Judgment* has been already referred to. See especially

the fact that he never sees merely color, but a colored shape
with boundaries (lines which have direction). As soon as a
sensation takes on any degree of definition or form, as soon as
it becomes an *object* of consciousness, it is perceptual intuition
and a possible object of the aesthetc attitude.

It is unnecessary to exhibit in concrete experience an exact
line between perceptual intuition and perception of fact, because
perceptions of fact, in adult life, always influence the data of
perceptual intuition. Do we see houses and trees and cats, in
all strictness, or do we see colored shapes that we take to be
houses and trees and cats? Strictly speaking, houses and trees
and cats are concepts; but that a colored shape is seen as a house
actually influences our apprehension of the color and the shape.[8]
It has been noted above that the visual field includes depth and
distance, although these are not strictly properties of any separate sensations. The depth and distance are part of the perceptual intuition of the field because of the way in which we are accustomed to interpret the sensations in terms of fact.

From the knowledge that perception of fact influences the
data of perceptual intuition, it might be deduced that even the
most elementary aesthetic experience is influenced in a most

Chapters VI, VII, and VIII of that work. In his later book, *Aesthetic Analysis*
(New York, 1936), there is a more elaborate treatment illustrated in Chapter III
by great detail from the musical scale. These intrinsic orders are the result of the
structural and qualitative relations which are given along with sensation.

[8] Simple examples of this influence can be found in such figures as the "shifting
staircase" or the "alternating cube" or the "double cross on a background," which
can be found in elementary psychology texts. Many such figures are given in
Köhler, *Gestalt Psychology* (New York, 1929), Chapters V and VI. Although the
purpose for which Köhler uses the figures is slightly different from that suggested
above, his whole treatment illustrates perfectly the extent to which our actual
apprehension of shape (in this instance) is influenced by conditions other than the
physical stimulus.

complex way by factors which themselves are not primarily aesthetic; and in due time the way this enters into the appreciation of aesthetic value must be examined. For the present, it is sufficient to say that within the object of the aesthetic attitude is included all that appears or seems to be immediately given in intuition.[9] The data of intuition are given in the sense that it is from them that the whole of actual experience— "thick experience"—starts. These data are what appears to be "objective" in experience, and behind them the mind cannot go except by reflective reasoning.

The aesthetic attitude is attention directed toward the appearance before the mind, no matter how that appearance comes to be there. Different conclusions concerning how it comes to be there may be reached by philosophical analysis, but these are not distinguished on the face of the perception. They can be discovered only as a result of the reflective method of philosophy. When D. W. Prall speaks of the object of the aesthetic experience as the "intuited surface of our world," [10] he seems to be calling attention to this fact that the aesthetic is that which is immediately given. "Given in perception" means "apprehended immediately" (that is, without mediation of other mental processes) as it appears.

---

[9] In truth, there could be no difference between what *is* given in intuition and what *appears* to be given, because the appearing is the being given.

[10] *Aesthetic Judgment,* p. 30. I prefer the expression "perceptual aspect" rather than "surface" because there are perceptual aspects of objects which are superficial and others which are not. "Surface" is metaphorical, hence open to misinterpretation.

6.

The perceptual imagination yields materials for the aesthetic experience. Works of art that present everything in absolute literal detail and leave no room for the play of the imagination seem often to be inferior for that reason. Yet one might ask, how this could be. If it is true that such works of art are inferior, how can it be explained in harmony with the view that the materials of the aesthetic experience are perceptual in character? How can one perceive what is not actually present? Details that are left to the imagination are not actually present.

The answer to these difficulties lies in the fact that the distinction between what is actual and what is imagined is not an intuitive distinction, but is intellectual. The terms "perception" and "perceptual grasp," in so far as they are used to refer only to perceptual intuition, include always both "actual" perception and the perceptual imagination. Psychologically considered, there is no absolute dividing line between the two. Both are equally the object of the aesthetic attitude. To distinguish between them requires the knowledge of abstract relations and consequences which are not immediately present in the perception itself. Only intellectual analysis can distinguish between the two; hence, the distinction is irrelevant to the aesthetic attitude.

All cognition of objects as facts involves more than is given in the present intuition. As has been pointed out above, a street car includes what one can do with it and what it can do to one. The veracity of perception can be determined only by this element, which goes beyond the present.[11] It has been brought out above that the aesthetic attitude is not directed toward future consequences or implications, but only toward what is immediately present, and that the aesthetic experience is not a kind of knowledge. If one knows anything about the veracity of perception, it is by means of the intellect. Without judgment, there is no question of veridical perception. Without the criticism of reason, there can be no error in perception, or "unreal" perception.

What is present to the perceptual imagination is as immediately given to intuition as what is present to "actual" perception. All this is to say that when one talks about veridical perception he is talking about the perception of fact, and not perceptual intuition. Therefore the distinction between veridical and erroneous perception has no significance for aesthetics. Perception of fact may be real or unreal, true or false; but perceptual intuition may not. It is what is given as it appears, and to predicate true or false of it has no significance.

7.

Pleasure and aesthetic materials. It has been often maintained that the materials of beauty necessarily must be sensuously agreeable. The relation, however, between sensuous agreeableness and pleasure in the aesthetic experience is the

---

[11] See C. I. Lewis, *Mind and the World Order*, New York, 1929, pp. 118 and 164.

same as that between sensation and perception. Pleasant sensation cannot be definitive of aesthetic material, because the aesthetic experience is perceptual. It is probable that there is always some sensuous content to perception, but the fact that this content may or may not be agreeable is not what makes the aesthetic experience what it is. Its agreeableness is not essential, although reason will be found later for holding that it is not irrelevant. As a matter of fact, it will be found that most of the sensuous materials of the aesthetic experience are pleasant.

This fact, that most of the sensuous materials are pleasant, has led many thinkers to suppose that the aesthetic experience is based on the awareness of pleasure. All pleasure, however, is not aesthetic, and it is necessary to find the special differentia of aesthetic pleasure. H. R. Marshall holds that that field of pleasure which is relatively permanent in revival can be characterized as aesthetic.[12] A more usual distinction, however, is to point out the difference between physical, bodily pleasures and aesthetic pleasures. Some pleasure is internal and subjective and is easily and unreflectively recognized as subjective. Therefore, it is not strictly common to others, or even communicable. Beauty, on the other hand, is felt to be more or less common or universal. This explanation goes back to Kant.[13] If one experiences beauty in a rose, he feels that others

---

[12] H. R. Marshall, *Pain, Pleasure and Aesthetics,* London and New York, 1894, pp. 151–153. Compare also Marshall's discussion of the connection between pleasure and the aesthetic experience in his *Aesthetic Principles,* New York, 1895, pp. 15–32.

[13] See the *Critique of Judgment.* Part I, Div. I, Sections 6–7. Bernard's translation, pp. 55–58.

must have the same satisfaction in it as himself. The difference between the pleasure of bodily feeling and the pleasure of beauty is the difference between that pleasure which is manifestly private and subjective and that pleasure which is common and seems to be objective. To paraphrase Santayana's definition of beauty, beauty is objectified pleasure.[14]

The view represented here by Kant and Santayana is true, but what it shows is that aesthetic pleasure is not pleasure in sensation alone, but pleasure in perception. All perception has an "objective reference," as has been pointed out above. This means only that in perception there seems to be something objective which is set over against it. There is a factor present which is not ordinarily localized in the body of the perceiver, but outside his body. This fact leads one to call it an object.[15] It makes no difference even though this object be intellectually appraised as imaginary or partly imaginary or illusory. Simple internal bodily sensations of comfort and agreeableness or of discomfort and pain are not usually taken up into perceptual complexes. Sensations as such are not the substance of aesthetic values, and aesthetic pleasure is not pleasure in sensation. If one sees that the aesthetic attitude is directed toward the data of perception and remembers that sensation is not the same as perception, it is not necessary to elaborate the "objectified nature of beauty." The kind of pleasure which is aesthetic is distinguished from that which is not by being pleasure in the data of perceptual intuition.

---

[14] G. Santayana, *The Sense of Beauty*, New York, 1896, pp. 47–49.

[15] By "object" here, I am, of course, not referring necessarily to a material entity, much less to a stone or a tree or a house. By "object" I mean whatever is presented to a mind.

It is theoretically unsatisfactory that the objectified nature of aesthetic pleasure (although it is true) should be the final criterion of aesthetic value, for then there would be no way of distinguishing some kinds of moral hedonists from lovers of beauty. To those philosophers who deny the validity of moral hedonism the distinction will be satisfactory. It is not an adequate distinction, however, if it is satisfactory only to those who hold a certain view in ethics or who refuse to hold it. The moral hedonist, in defining the good as pleasure, may think of a pleasure which is just as universal, communicable, and objectified as is Santayana's beauty. If he is a Utilitarian, he does; and yet he need not hold that all moral value is only a disguised form of aesthetic value—that the only goodness is beauty.

8.

Emotion and aesthetic materials. The same sort of error which has led some to say that the material of the aesthetic experience is whatever is sensuously pleasant has led others to say that this material must be evocative of emotion. It is true that the aesthetic experience is usually one of heightened emotional stimulation, but this fact does not make emotion definitive of the aesthetic experience. Sensuous agreeableness, aesthetic perception, and emotion are three very different things even though in concrete experience all three may occur together and, in fact, be inseparable from each other except by way of analysis. Sensation is the content of perception, and emotions are caused by perception. A few primitive emotional states may be caused by sensation; for example, fear by a loud noise. But the bulk of adult reactions is highly conditioned, and the emotions of adult life are aroused by perceptions. The great degree to which the powers of perception are active in the aesthetic experience will almost invariably arouse an emotional response in the ordinary person. Consequently, the aesthetic experience will usually be emotional, and it will be found later that this also is not irrelevant to aesthetic value, but it is not an essential or definitive characteristic.

The ordinary perceptions of adult life are perceptions of fact. These, as has been shown, are more than aesthetic perceptions, but they are based on aesthetic perceptions. The same process of conditioning which makes perceptions of fact stimuli for the emotions also makes the perceptual intuitions which are fundamental to these perceptions of fact stimuli for the emotions. These perceptual intuitions, when one is in the aesthetic attitude, do not have the practical, moral, and intellectual significance that they ordinarily have (that is, when they are taken up into perceptions of fact). They do not call forth the same bodily responses. Part of the characteristic flavor of what we call a specific emotion lies in the bodily responses to the stimuli that arouse the emotions.[16] These bodily responses are absent or subordinated in the aesthetic experience; hence the emotional states which accompany the aesthetic experience seem vague and disembodied. They lack part of the

---

[16] This view has been held in one form or another ever since the time of the original James-Lange theory of the emotions. Exactly what the detailed form is, is of no consequence here.

conditions that ordinarily give them their characteristic flavor.

The observation of this fact, that the emotion which may be aroused in the aesthetic experience is different in quality from the emotions aroused in the ordinary course of practical life, led, perhaps, to Aristotle's catharsis theory of tragedy. At any rate, it is the basis for whatever truth there may be in the catharsis theory. It has led many contemporary writers to define the aesthetic experience in terms of emotion.[17]

These writers have been led to the view that emotion is definitive of the aesthetic experience by two considerations. As was pointed out in Chapter I of the present work, the experience of value is immediate apprehension, which is more akin to an effective state than to intellectual or cognitive activity. As is pointed out directly above, the aesthetic experience is usually accompanied by emotions, and these emotions are without some of their characteristic components; therefore, they seem to be peculiarly set off from "the common emotions of life." Consequently, it seems that the aesthetic experience can be defined in terms of these peculiar emotions. These two considerations, when not distinguished from each other, seem to indicate "an aesthetic emotion."

This position indicates a lack of understanding of what psychology says the emotions are. In the first place, psychology long ago gave up the habit of speaking of broad undifferentiated affective states as emotions.[18] When psychology uses the term "emotion," it always has in mind some kind of emotion—an emotion, such as fear or anger or the tender feeling,

---

[17] For example, Clive Bell. See especially *Art*, London, 1914, pp. 6, 8, and 28.
[18] Compare C. C. Pratt, *The Meaning of Music*, New York, 1931, p. 177.

or some compound of the more elementary emotions. The fundamental feeling of excitement is basic to all the specific emotions, but what distinguishes one specific emotion from another may be overt bodily actions that are extraneous to the fundamental feeling of excitement. A specific emotion is stimulated by a certain kind of objective situation which produces definite bodily and glandular reactions, and is, perhaps, connected with some impulsive or instinctive tendency. Descriptions of "the aesthetic emotion" do not fit into this scheme at all. Even if the aesthetic experience could be called an affective state, it would be so in a much more fundamental and less delineated way than are the emotions. "The aesthetic emotion" is much too vague a term to be theoretically adequate as a basis for an understanding of aesthetics.[19]

If the basis of the aesthetic experience were "an aesthetic emotion," still this emotion would have to be differentiated from moral and practical emotions ("the common emotions of life"). The only way adequately to do this is by recourse to the conditions wherein these emotions are aroused: the attitude

---

[19] Much of the above criticism is directed at Clive Bell and that school of art critics influenced by him. It is interesting to note that Roger Fry, although he often has much in common with Bell, is one of the most competent of contemporary critics of painting. In his earlier book, *Vision and Design* (London, 1920), he often fell into the language of "the aesthetic emotion," but in *Transformations* (London, 1926) he modified his theory to say that aesthetic apprehension is the apprehension of relations (*Transformations,* p. 3). Fry does not explain clearly and definitely what kinds of relations he means, but he excludes conceptual relations. Owing to his preoccupation with pictorial and plastic art, he sometimes seems to envisage these relations as pre-eminently spatial, but this is not all he means, because he applies the dictum to literature and music. Fry's position can be elucidated and justified by the interpretation that these relations are perceptual relations: the structural and qualitative relations between possible sense data which are given along with those data.

of the individual and the nature of the stimulus. The criterion of what is aesthetic here, as well as what is aesthetic in general, is perceptual grasp. The difference between the aesthetic emotions and the moral or practical emotions is that the aesthetic accompany apprehension in the aesthetic attitude—apprehension of perceptual data for their own sake.

9.

Feeling and aesthetic materials. Feeling has been declared by many writers to be definitive of the aesthetic experience, but this procedure is neither clear nor precise. The term "feeling" has various meanings: it may be used as more or less synonymous with "emotion"; or it may be used only in reference to pleasure and pain; or it may be used to mean sensibility, especially the sense of touch; or it may be used to denote any fundamental state of awareness whose character cannot be described fully and adequately by the discursive intellect. It has been used in all of these meanings in the history of aesthetics. Often, when it is used explicitly in one meaning, a specious reliance upon the other meanings makes it plausible. If it is used to mean "emotion," it does not yield a satisfactory theory of aesthetics, for, as has been shown in the preceding section, the assumption that there is a specific aesthetic emotion is based upon a confusion; and the view that all aesthetic experience is definable in terms of emotion—different unique emotions each peculiar to its own aesthetic object—is likewise based on the failure to discriminate between the moment of perceptual intuition and the emotion which may be aroused by such intuition.[20]

Early in the history of modern aesthetic theory, Kant, in the *Critique of Judgment,* defined the aesthetic by means of feeling, but he was explicit that it was in the hedonic sense he used the term. Rarely does he use "feeling" outside the whole phrase "the feeling of pleasure and pain," or at least "the feeling of pleasure." Kant's reference of the aesthetic judgment to the feeling of pleasure and pain is an important part of the architectonic of his whole philosophical system, and the reference to pleasure and pain seems to give an explanatory principle primarily because of the place which his aesthetic theory plays in his whole system. One should not expect the problems of aesthetics to be solved in a satisfactory manner when approached from the standpoint of an interest not primarily in them but in other problems of philosophy. Kant locates incorrectly the place of the feeling of pleasure and pain in the aesthetic experience because he was interested not so much in expounding an adequate theory of aesthetics as he was in completing the structure of his philosophic system. The feelings of pleasure and pain (or more accurately, of displeasure) are very important to a complete definition of aesthetic value, as will be brought out later, but this is no reason for defining the aesthetic experience primarily in these terms.[21]

---

[20] For an excellent exposition of such a theory see C. J. Ducasse, *The Philosophy of Art,* New York, 1929. Ducasse's theory seems to me in the last analysis to come down to introspective data which I, for one, cannot verify. See p. 199 of his book.

[21] I feel that the place of Kant in the history of aesthetics is of utmost importance. The theory of aesthetics contained in the present study owes much to the insights of Kant, and in its emphasis on perception as the basis of the aesthetic experience it has much in common with the beginnings of modern aesthetics. Nevertheless,

The term "feeling" refers to affective states when used both in the sense of emotion and in the hedonic sense. The affective meaning of "feeling" may be strikingly contrasted with the meaning in which it refers to sensibility by noting that the terms "apathetic" and "anaesthetic" both mean "without feeling," but they are by no means synonymous. If "feeling" is used in aesthetic theory not in the affective sense but in the sense of a state of consciousness, the distinctive character of which is not fully comprehended by the discursive intellect, then it is simply an indefinite term to denote vaguely what has been developed into the concept of perceptual intuition in the present chapter. This "feeling" is perceptual grasp for which there may be no corresponding complete understanding: an awareness, either vague or clear, which is not cognitive. Perceptual intuition *is* feeling in this sense. It is the awareness of data immediately and directly present to the mind. Perceptual intuition is fundamental to all aesthetic experience, and all aesthetic value is to be defined by reference to it. To use the term "feeling" to denote this concept is to engender confusion. "Feeling" has been so widely used both with this meaning and to denote affective experience that its use in either sense alone is not advisable. If it is used, the theory which makes it definitive derives specious plausibility from its ambiguity.

I feel that there are inconsistencies and irrelevancies in Kant's theory, most of which can be traced to his endeavor to harmonize the disparate realms of the pure and of the practical reason. To argue this point at this place would be a digression, but I think it is of great importance; hence the discussion is given in full in Appendix B,

10.

Summary. In the last two chapters it has been shown that the aesthetic attitude is the attitude wherein attention is directed toward perceptual data, and that the object of this attitude is whatever is immediately present to consciousness through perceptual intuition. Perception is the activity which yields the materials of the aesthetic experience. "Aesthetic," wherever the term may be used and whatever it may qualify, means "perceptual" (always, it must be remembered, having reference primarily to perceptual intuition). The aesthetic experience, fundamentally, is the experience of perceptual apprehension—perceptual grasp. It is true that the aesthetic experience was characterized as an experience of value in the first chapter of the present study, but in the light of the last two chapters it is apparent that in so far as any value can be called aesthetic value, it is that value which is to be found in the data of perception. Therefore, the experience of this value will be found only in the perceptual grasp of that which is before consciousness as its object.

Aesthetic experience means perceptual experience; aesthetic value means perceptual value; aesthetic pleasure means perceptual pleasure (but this is not synonymous with sensuous pleasure); and if one uses the term "aesthetic perception," it means perceptual intuition emphatically distinguished from the perception of fact. It is true that in ordinary speech the term "aesthetic" means "having positive aesthetic value," and it was so used in the first chapter of the present study. Before positive aesthetic value can be defined, however, the generic concept of value which can be either positive or negative must be defined; and before aesthetic value can be defined the most fundamental meaning of the term "aesthetic" must be determined. This has now been done; but before going on to the nature of the value, the next chapter will investigate further aesthetic form; that is, those given relations and structure which make possible the perceptual grasp of a complex subject.

CHAPTER IV

Aesthetic Form

1.

The nature of aesthetic form. It was remarked in the preceding chapter that, in perception, structural and qualitative relations between sense data are given along with that data. These relations are the basis of aesthetic form. Aesthetic form is the organization of perceptual materials according to those structural and qualitative relations which are given in immediate apprehension. The basis of all aesthetic experience is perceptual grasp, and this grasp is the apprehension of the materials *as they are formally related.* Form is to be found wherever there is perception, and thus wherever there is aesthetic experience; but this form may be little or greatly complex, and may be less or more adequately grasped. An inquiry into the principles of aesthetic form is an investigation into the way that the given structural and qualitative relations enter into and make possible the perceptual grasp of a complex object.

The aesthetic attitude has been defined without excluding any of the data of perceptual intuition; hence it may be said that the quality essential to the aesthetic object is simply that it be perceptible. The nature of the object of the aesthetic experience is that it may be grasped in perception. Not all complex objects are grasped in perception with equal ease. Those structural relations which give rise to rhythm, pattern, proportion, and balance, and those qualitative relations which underlie much that is called harmony make possible the perceptual grasp of a complex object. When complex materials are given in these relations, the perceptual grasp of them may be relatively complete and adequate in spite of the complexity.

This is the explanation of the role played by rhythm, proportion, and balance in the aesthetic experience. These are structural elements. They are objective. They are the names for those relations which render the perceptual grasp of a complex object possible. It is so apparent that these characteristics are essential to the nature of beautiful objects that beauty has often been naïvely identified with them. Theories of aesthetics which suppose that value can be defined in wholly objective terms attempt to define beauty by means of the "golden section," or "dynamic symmetry," or a serpentine line. But these are not beauty. They are merely the objective factors in many of the situations in which beauty is experienced. Rhythm, proportion, balance, and so forth, are not aesthetic value, but they are important factors in the determination of that value because they are the structural principles which make the perceptual grasp of a complex object possible.

2.

Perceptual grasp illustrated by simple patterns. If two or three dots are put on a piece of paper, they are grasped perceptually at once. That is, they are seen, and all there is to see about them is seen. If the number of dots is increased to four or five, adult perception grasps them completely, but that of a child does not. Even four dots arranged haphazardly are too complex for the child's undeveloped powers of perception. It is apparent that his grasp is not complete because he apprehends no difference between the group of four and a group of five. If twelve or fourteen dots are put down haphazardly, adult perception may not be able to grasp them. But if they are arranged so that apprehension seizes them by breaking them up into similar perceptual elements, each of which can be grasped easily, then the whole can be grasped.

This is even more apparent if the number of dots (that is, the complexity of the situation) is increased. Take, for example, twenty-five dots and arrange them so that they cannot be apprehended in similar simple perceptual elements; that is, arrange them haphazardly. (See Figure 1.) These are not grasped as a unified group by perception. But if the twenty-five dots are arranged so that they can be perceived in simple groups which are similar to each other, an immediate grasp is possible. (See Figure 2.) If one dot were missing or in a

slightly different position in the first (haphazard) group, the
detail might not be noticed (that is, enter into the perception
of the situation) and the differ-
ence between the original and the
supposed copy might not be apparent without a close or detailed
examination involving some process of mediation such as counting
or measuring. This would be intellectual and would necessitate
an arbitrary isolation of parts

Figure 1.

from each other. Such a process would become more necessary
as the situation became more complex. In the perception of
the patterned group, however, the grasp is complete and immediate. The whole twenty-five dots are one thing. There is
a high degree of discrimination between this and other groups.

Figure 2.

This discrimination is a witness
to the completeness of the perceptual grasp. Counting, or any
process of mediation, is not necessary. The situation is seen as
a whole without the intervention
of any reasoning process. The
groups of Figures 3 and 4 are seen
to be different from the group
of Figure 2 without respect to
whether they contain more, fewer, or the same number of dots.

The last three figures are patterned groups, and this is what
patterned means: the whole is composed of parts, each of which

can be grasped in its entirety by immediate perception, and the parts are similar enough to each other in their structure so that the whole itself is grasped in perception. The pattern depends upon given structural relations between the parts of an object. These relations make possible the perceptual grasp of the object. When a situation becomes too complex to be grasped, it becomes disorderly; if relations are apparent which enable perception to grasp it, it has order and pattern.[1]

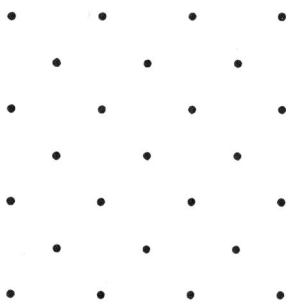

Figure 3.

Such perceptual grasp is aesthetic, and the ordering or structure of the parts is aesthetic form. The grasp is not cognitive or intellectual; it is apprehension, not understanding. Figures are used in geometry, and graphs in statistics and logic to reinforce the intellectual understanding by aesthetic apprehension. The understanding may be complete in itself. Figures are not necessary to the rigorous proof of a geometric system. But the understanding alone is often weak, and the aesthetic apprehension is more primitive; it is more primitive both in an evolutionary sense and analytically. Hence, although the fig-

Figure 4.

---

[1] I am, of course, not using "pattern" in the way a dressmaker might use it, but in the sense in which one would speak of "the pattern on the wall paper."

ures are not essential to the proofs in geometry and logic, they may be a great help in obtaining a mastery of these subjects.

3.

The nature of rhythm. The best example of the fundamental law of the perceptual grasp of a complex object is rhythm. Rhythm is the temporal patterning of an object of perception. In so far as all apprehension is in time, it may be said that rhythm is fundamental to all aesthetic form. Complete apprehension is limited by the "span of attention," which is not great, and this limitation is such that if a simple temporal object is to be grasped, it must fall not far beyond the limits of the "specious present." One cannot grasp that which in its temporal manifestation is too complex (that is, composed of a large number of elements spread over a large amount of time) unless the complexity can be divided into a number of groups, each of which is relatively simple within itself, and each of which is similar enough to the others so that the qualitative relation between them can be grasped immediately. In this case there is perceptual grasp of the whole.

A simple illustration will suffice to show how the grasp of a complex temporal object is accomplished by means of rhythmic patterns. If a bell is struck, or any tapping sound is made in more or less rapid succession two or three times, the grasp of the whole is complete and immediate. It is not necessary for the hearer of the sounds to count them to be able to perceive them as a group of a certain kind. He can, perhaps, reproduce them, or recognize at once, without intellectual analysis, any alteration in a repetition of the group. His perceptual grasp is complete. He hears the sounds, and he hears all there is to hear about them as a whole. If, however, the sounds are made a large number of times, say twenty-nine times, it is not probable that the perceptual grasp of the group is at all complete. The hearer may count the sounds, but this would give him an intellectual, not a perceptual grasp. If he does not count them, he does not have any complete grasp. The group might be changed, some beats added or some taken away, and he would never perceive the difference.

If the succession of twenty-nine beats is now changed so that there is a slight pause after every fourth beat, or so that every fourth beat is stressed, it is easy for the listener to grasp the whole as a unit. He now recognizes a certain character in the whole such that he would at once perceive any alteration in it. If a few beats were added, he would recognize this new group to be different from the old. He is apt to say that he "feels" a difference between them, but the term "feeling" here is used in a very vague sense. It refers to perceptual grasp, for which there is no corresponding intellectual grasp. He may be able to reproduce the group exactly despite the fact that he has never counted the number of beats in it. His apprehension seizes four groups of four each. Then again, four groups of four each are started, but the last is not quite completed.[2] In case there is some slight rhythmic pattern im-

---

[2] Although I have spoken of four groups in order to describe the situation, I do not imply that there is any counting here. The grasp is qualitative, not primarily quantitative.

parted to the succession of beats, and in case they are rather rapid, it is possible for most persons, with a little practice, to grasp as a unit as many as 256 beats.

In this example, the structural basis of a compound pattern is actually present in the object presented. This is not always or necessarily the case. Some persons always hear a succession of sounds, even though it is perfectly regular and without accent, as if it were broken up into recurrent rhythmic groups. A clock strikes eleven times, and such a person hears it in groups; either two groups of four each and then not quite another, or three groups of three each and then not quite another. It does not matter in the example of rhythmic apprehension whether the basis of the compound pattern is actually present in the stimulus or is only "heard in" by the listener. It is simpler, of course, where there is a basis in the physical stimulus; but the person who becomes expert in hearing rhythmic groups "into" a succession of sounds grasps the whole as a unit just as does the person who is dependent upon the physical basis. Compound rhythms, whether they have a physical basis or not, take their significance from the way that perception grasps a complex temporal object.

The rhythmic apprehension of still more complex objects may be complete and immediate. In the above example, the first actual rhythmic structure is the regular recurrence of beats in time. When one beat in four is stressed, a compound rhythm is introduced. Each group of four is a unit in a larger structure. Combinations of one to two, or one to three, or one to four rhythms are common to all the temporal arts.

More elaborate combinations called "complex," or "cross,"

rhythms are found when one fundamental measure is divided up into two lesser beats by one division, and at the same time into three by another; or into three by one and four by another. There may seem to be an actual "pulling of the two against the three" or the three against the four, especially if, as in orchestration, instruments of very different timbre and pitch are sounding the different beats. It will be observed that in addition to the cross pulling of the rhythm, a complex recurring pattern of sounds is created. It is often the case that intricate-sounding rhythmic patterns are merely the patterns of these complex or cross rhythms. Sometimes the intellectual analysis of a complex pattern is very difficult even though the perceptual grasp of it is complete and immediate. The fact that one can produce or reproduce it without any understanding of what analysis shows it to be is evidence of its complete grasp by perception.

To take an example: most persons, if unpracticed and if their attention were directed only to the control of the muscles, would find it difficult to make one hand tap twice while the other taps three times, or to make one tap three while the other taps four. If one hears another do it, however, he apprehends it at once: he hears the pattern and may be able to reproduce it with his two hands without difficulty. The patterns of three to four and four to five rhythms are relatively easy to grasp, but more complex combinations cannot be apprehended without practice, and the limit of complexity is soon reached. The simpler combinations that can be grasped at once can be varied in many ways and different effects be produced by ellipsis of some beats, by doubling some, and by syncopation. The most elaborate temporal structures of music, poetry, and the dance are built up in this way.

Although rhythm is a measured recurrence in time, and the apprehension of rhythmic patterns is the fundamental principle of the perceptual grasp of temporal objects, the word "rhythm" is often applied also to spatial objects. Spatial rhythm is spoken of in the criticism of painting and sculpture and architecture, and perhaps correctly, for the apprehension of complex objects in space takes time. Space may be there all at once, and reflectively it may be necessary to think of it there all at once, but no one ever perceived it so. Except in very small and simple sections, there is no perceptual grasp of it all at once.[3] As the eye moves over a composition or an architectural structure, recurrent lines or masses, spaced at intervals so that the apprehension of them is rhythmical, make the composition rhythmical. This is very closely allied to the principles of proportion and balance in spatial composition.

4.

The nature of proportion and balance. The spatial patterning of an object gives rise to the qualities which in the visual arts are called proportion and balance. The first example of the patterning of a complex object of perception given above, the example of the dots, was spatial, and is the simplest case

---

[3] I should not need to call attention to the fact that I have not been using the word "immediate" to mean "all at once," but have been using it in its more fundamental sense of "not mediated." Temporal mediation is only one kind of mediation.

of spatial patterning. A further complication is to be found in the abstract line design. If such a design is at all elaborate, there are structural relations between the parts such that the parts fall into simple groups, and there is a qualitative relation of similarity or easy contrast between the groups. For example, in an intricate arabesque, there are many recurrences of the same simple structure varied by the simple contrast introduced by bilateral symmetry. The whole design is composed of parts, each structurally simple in itself, and each part is in a simple qualitative relation to the other parts and to the whole. When these relationships are grasped, the design appears as a unit. When they are not present, that is, when there is no relation of similarity or simple contrast between the parts, or when the perception of some parts leads the observer to expect others that are not there, then the principles of proportion and balance have not been observed. The grasp of the composition is not unified. It is not a whole.

There are commonly observed rules in design concerning the use of curved and flowing lines and the use of straight lines and angles. If both kinds of lines are used in the same design, there must be some kind of transition between them. A rule like this is the recognition in practice that the qualitative relations between the parts of a complex object must be such that an immediate grasp is possible. All the rules of proportion and balance are based upon the same formal relations: those which are conducive to the perceptual grasp of a complex object.

In pointing out these principles, aesthetics must not be understood to be laying down rules that the practitioner of the arts must obey. It is not the function of aesthetics to lay down rules, but only to find the theoretic principles of explanation for those practices which the artist finds aesthetically effective. Furthermore, it is probable that no absolute rules can be laid down. What the artist finds effective at one time and under one set of conditions might not be effective under altered conditions. Objects are perceived in habitual ways, and as habit changes, it may be that the actual conditions of perceptual grasp change correspondingly. In such cases, the rules would have to change, or art would become aesthetically sterile.

The use of color complicates the problem of spatial patterning, because different colors have different "weights," to use the technical language of the colorist. The use of color may throw out of balance a composition which, considered merely as a line design, might be in balance. This is because the perception of spaces is influenced by the color that those spaces have. Experiment has established, for example, that a white spot on a black background looks larger than a black spot of exactly the same size on a white background. Experiment has also shown that the juxtaposition of various colors makes the perception of each of them different. They may differ both in size and in degree of saturation, both of which affect the "weight" of the color. All of these differences are differences in the given structural and qualitative relations that are at the bottom of aesthetic form.

The use of the third dimension also introduces a new complication into the principles of proportion and balance, because a pattern is perceived differently if it is seen in perspective.

The third dimension may be introduced by projection onto a flat surface, as it is in painting, or it may be introduced in actuality, as it is in sculpture and architecture. The third dimension influences the proportion and balance of a composition only in so far as it actually affects perception, but the perception of lines and colors as composing a perspective is quite different from the perception of those same lines and colors as flat. [4]

When painting is even to a slight degree representational, the lines and colors seem to fall together into groups, because they represent objects which within our experience are composed of such groupings. This kind of grouping and patterning is not strictly an element of aesthetic form dependent only on the nature of the object. It is dependent upon the observer's past experience, but nevertheless, is very influential in determining the grasp of the form. Within past experience, the lines and colors have always fallen together in a certain way, and so, by long familiarity, they are apprehended immediately as a group, although in their structural nature they may be very complex. For example, a face is a very complex visual object, but the ease of recognition of those we have seen often or intensely is an evidence of the high degree of perceptual grasp we may have of faces. The balance and proportion of representational painting depends to a large degree on the perceptual grasp of familiar groupings of visual elements.

---

[4] Examples of "optical illusions" due to the introduction of perspective can be found in any elementary psychology text. These are striking examples of the perceptual difference between a flat and a perspective design.

5.

Formal considerations in harmony. Harmony is not strictly a principle of aesthetic form, for it cannot be defined without reference to what gives pleasure, and it involves questions of taste. Although harmony is not wholly formal, nevertheless, given, qualitative, formal relations between sense data underlie much that we call harmony. Thus, a pattern of colors in red and purple is not the same aesthetic form as the same pattern (defined in terms of space alone) in red and green, and the reason for this is that the given qualitative relation between red and purple is not the same as that between red and green. A piece of music played in one tempo is not the same aesthetic form as when it is played in a radically different tempo, and again the difference is due to the altered qualitative relations.

To say that two things (colors, tones, persons, or anything else) are harmonious does not mean much more than to say that they go well together, and to say that they are aesthetically harmonious means that they are perceived well together. As was said above, this is partly dependent upon our habits of perceiving and what we are accustomed to, but it is also dependent on objective conditions which are given in the experience of perceiving. It has been brought out that in order for perception to grasp a complex situation, the complexity must be such that it is made up of parts between which there are qualitative relations of easy similarity or contrast so that the way they go together to make a whole is immediately apparent. This latter consideration is the formal element which is at the bottom of much that we call harmony. The parts of a complex whole must be such that a perceptual grasp of the whole is **possible.**

For example, musical intervals which are consonant are made up of tones which have very specific likenesses: they have overtones in common. To our ears it seems apparent that an octave of any given tone is very much like the given tone, and the reason for this probably lies in the fact that most of the tones of our experience are produced by vibrating strings or columns of air, and we rarely hear the given tone without its octave being included within it as an integral part. Similarly, the tonic triad is harmonious for the reason that when we hear the fundamental tone the octaves of the third and the fifth are already faintly contained within it. The qualitative similarity here goes back to structural relations. It is true that one may not be aware and never be aware of the fact that when he hears the fundamental it contains as overtones octaves of the third and the fifth. The qualitative similarity is given, however, even though the reason for it may not be superficially apparent.

The relations between the parts of a complex whole must be those of easy similarity or contrast in order for the parts to appear harmonious, and this has been found to be the case in simple tones that are harmonious when taken together. Any two tones which have important overtones in common are harmonious. The perception of each part enhances the perception of the others,

In actual musical compositions, however, the greatest dissonances may be used with fine effects. In dissonances, tones are found together between which there is no easy relation of similarity, but this does not contradict the general rule. The dissonant chord is not a self-sufficient structural element. It is a part of a larger temporal group completed by the resolution. This larger group supersedes the single chord, and the easy similarity between the parts which is needed to make a single chord harmonious is supplanted by the temporal contrast given in the movement of the resolution.[5]

In colors, those colors related to each other by simple relations of hue, chroma (or saturation), and value (or intensity) are usually found to be harmonious. It is likewise true that colors which are complementary to each other in hue, if the chroma and value are not too different, are harmonious. This is because the nature of color vision is such that the specific quality of each of two complementary hues is perceived more clearly when these two hues are in juxtaposition. The two hues mutually intensify each other; that is, the perception of each enhances that of the other: they are harmonious. Of course, such a harmony is vivid, for it is based on contrast and intensification. If one of the colors is neutralized a little, however, that is, if its saturation is slightly decreased, the harmony becomes softer because the mutual intensification is diminished, although it is still there. If the loss of saturation in only one of the colors is carried too far, the colors become less harmo-

---

[5] I am aware that what appears a satisfactory resolution at one time to one will not at another time to others. Again questions of taste complicate the situation but must be postponed until we have laid the foundation necessary for their consideration.

nious.   Two colors, both of which are of a low degree of saturation, give quieter harmonies because the contrast offered by
mutual intensification is supplanted by the similarity in the
grayness of the colors.

The same caution must be observed here as was observed
above.   Absolute rules of harmony cannot be made, because
in the first place harmony is not strictly a principle of form,
and in the second, even those considerations which are formal
are aesthetic only because they are conducive to perceptual
grasp, and the conditions and habits of perception may change
from time to time.

6.

Unity in variety.   Aesthetic form is that definition of an
object which can be grasped by perception.   The grasp is immediate and therefore a unity.   But the object as a whole may
be very complex.   If it is, this complexity must exhibit relations which make a unified grasp possible.   A very simple
object may be grasped without difficulty, but it is not apt to
awaken much interest in the apprehending individual.   A very
complex object has all the conditions to arouse great interest,
but to grasp it in perception is difficult.   If the complexity is
presented in such a way as to make a grasp possible, then
there are present the conditions both of interest and apprehension.   Rhythm, proportion, balance, some of the conditions of harmony, and so forth, are all factors which enable a
complex object to be caught up in the unity of apprehension.

Aesthetic form has often been defined in the history of aesthetics as unity in variety, or unity in multiplicity, or unity in a manifold.[6] And it may be seen that aesthetic form is such; but this formula does not go very far in explaining either the nature or the principles of aesthetic form. The unity is the unity of perceptual grasp; the object is apprehended as one object. In the aesthetic attitude, one is not attending to the parts of the object or to the details of the form of the object by themselves. In fact, within the aesthetic attitude the parts do not exist separately. One apprehends simply the total effect, the whole. He grasps the unity which may, within another mental attitude, be analyzed into separate parts. The unity is the grasp. The variety is the varied parts of a complex whole. The unity is the apprehension, the variety is the condition of interest. The unity in variety is the way that the complexity is gathered up into a whole by the powers of perception.

One has not discovered aesthetic value when he has discovered unity in variety. Aesthetic form is not aesthetic value. It is one of the conditions of the existence of the value. The principles of form are not the principles of value. To say that an object is grasped by perception is not to say that it has positive aesthetic value. That which has the highest positive value usually will not be perfectly and completely grasped because it will not be simple enough. Like *Hamlet,* it may be such that every time we return to it we find something new. Its variety may seem inexhaustible, but whatever grasp

---

[6] Cf. Santayana, *The Sense of Beauty,* pp. 95 ff.

we have of it is sufficient unto the time thereof. Aesthetic value means perceptual value; therefore the object which has aesthetic value must be perceived, and the principles which are conducive to perceptual grasp are necessary conditions for the existence of the value. This is not all, however, for values are experienced as less or more intense, and there are positive and negative values. The relation between aesthetic form and aesthetic value cannot be made clear until all the conditions of the experience of value are understood. The next chapter will go on to this problem.

CHAPTER V

The Evaluating Factor

1.

Both polarity and intensity of values are explained by a measure for the comparison of values. Value is polar. That is, there are positive values and negative values (or disvalues). The terms "value" and "valuable" are ordinarily used to denote only the positive values, and for this reason perhaps it is better to speak of values and disvalues. But there is a need for a generic term to cover both value and disvalue, and as there is no such term in the English language, "value" is used both in the generic sense and in the sense of indicating the positive pole. No confusion need arise, however, because the context always clearly indicates whether the term is being used in the broader or narrower sense, and in cases where the positive value is taken only as an example of value in general, what is said of it applies also to the general concept. Where this is not the case, and the negative sense, the disvalue, is excluded, it may easily be indicated.

The disvalue is not merely a lack of value any more than debts are merely a lack of money. Something which is economically harmful is in a specific sense diametrically opposed to what is economically beneficial, though in a general sense it is similar in being still economic. It is not only a lack of benefit, for generically it is the same; specifically, however, it is not only different from benefit, but is its exact opposite. All value is polar in this way, and the polarity is expressed in the common antitheses of beauty and ugliness, good and evil, benefit and hurt, wisdom and folly, and so on. The polarity is a given datum in the apprehension of value. That is, values are immediately apprehended in accordance with their given nature as positive or negative: the experience of beauty is one experience and the experience of ugliness another. The values bear their character as positive or negative on their faces.[1]

Values also differ in intensity. The experience which a lover of music has when he hears Bach's Mass in B minor superbly rendered is quite different from that which he has when he hears an ordinary piece of music. The difference between the two experiences is to a large degree a difference in intensity. This is why he calls the second-mentioned piece "ordinary." Some values are more intense than others, and the intensity

---

[1] Of course, it is true here as in many other cases that the determination of which of the polar opposites shall be called "positive" and which "negative" is a matter largely of verbal and practical convenience. The negative is as "positive" in its own way as is the positive.

is a datum of the experience. It is the business of a study of aesthetics to render coherently intelligible all the conditions of the actual experience. The intensity is a datum, and a theoretic principle for the measure of the intensity must be found.

At least in the case of aesthetic value, the polarity and the intensity are not unrelated to each other. Intensity is rendered intelligible by comparison of one value with another. Without the ability to compare, it is possible that intensity would still be a datum, but it would have no meaning and no intelligible explanation. The same general truth holds of polarity. Polar terms are relative to each other, and a comparison is a recognition of the relation. This does not mean that when one is experiencing any given intensity of value he is explicitly comparing that value to some other either more or less intense; or that when he is experiencing a positive or a negative value he explicitly has in mind its relative antithesis. The actual comparison is not a datum of the experience, and if carried out, is extraneous to the experience; but nevertheless, the ability to compare may be what renders the datum intelligible.

There is some condition in the nature of the experience of aesthetic value which determines the intensity and polarity of that value. The intelligibility of intensity and polarity depends upon comparison; therefore, if one can find a factor by reference to which values can be compared and measured in terms of one another, one can explain the data of intensity and polarity. It then becomes apparent what place they have in relation to all the other parts of the aesthetic experience. This is true even though the explicit comparison and measurement are not integral parts of the experience of aesthetic value itself.

The factor by means of which the comparison between values is made may be called the evaluating factor. It has been pointed out above that to value and to evaluate are different. Valuing is an immediate experience. It is not intellectual or cognitive. Evaluation, however, is cognitive. To evaluate is to make a judgment concerning the value of anything. There are many occasions to make judgments concerning values, but the most usual undoubtedly is the occasion to compare values—to think of one thing as more or less valuable than another. Such comparisons can be made only in terms of judgments concerning the value of each of the members of the comparison; that is, only in terms of evaluations. Hence, the basis for comparison is an evaluating factor.

Before the nature of aesthetic value is fully understood, this evaluating factor must be determined. It is the basis of comparison, and renders the intensity and polarity of values intelligible. More of it makes the value more valuable, and less makes it less valuable. Its presence makes the value positive, and the presence of its relative opposite makes the value negative. Of course, any basis of comparison or reason for comparing values is irrelevant if it is not compatible with the conditions of the aesthetic attitude, for only aesthetic values are under consideration. It is not necessary, however, to be aware of the criterion by means of which one values much or little before he can value much or little, any more than it is necessary to understand the nature of value before he can value. The valuing comes first. The fact that one does value things much or little is the consideration which leads him to attempt to find the criterion whereby he does so.

2.

The nature of intrinsic value. The way to determine the evaluating factor for aesthetic value is to examine the aesthetic experience and the nature of intrinsic value, and to see what in the psychological makeup of the individual leads him to value some things more intensely than others. It has been noted above that values can be classified according to their interest and object into moral, religious, political, economic, aesthetic, and so on. Values can be classified also according to their structure, and this gives the distinction between intrinsic and instrumental values.

An obvious illustration of the difference between intrinsic and instrumental values lies in the fact that one sometimes considers a disagreeable medicine valuable. It is valuable, not in itself, but for the sake of the health induced. Health has an intrinsic value. It is good to be healthy just for the sake of being healthy. In so far, however, as one values his health in order to accomplish something by means of it (like supporting his family), he is valuing it also instrumentally. To know the nature of intrinsic value is important because aesthetic values are intrinsic.

The ordinary elucidation of the distinction between intrinsic and instrumental values is that intrinsic value is valuable as an end in itself, but an instrumental value takes its value from the fact that it is a means to a valuable end. The instrumental value, *qua* instrumental, has no value in itself. It is an instrument in reaching something else which is valuable and borrows whatever value it seems to have from this fact.

This ordinary explanation is clear enough for practical purposes, but it is not very exact. G. E. Moore, in attempting to reach a more precise statement, defines an intrinsic value as a value which any object would have even if nothing else existed.[2] Moore is apparently led to this definition by the observation that value, if intrinsic, seems peculiarly internal to the object that has it. This observation is true, but the definition follows from it only on the basis of Moore's view that value is a peculiar property of an object, simple and undefinable, which the object has without regard to any sensibility.[3] If intrinsic value is value which an object has as an end in itself, and if value is a real property (or the function of a real property) which an object has independent of anything else, then it would have its intrinsic value *even if nothing else existed*.

This definition is not satisfactory unless value is wholly "objective," that is, unless value is a real property of objects or the function of real properties. The present theory holds that

---

[2] G. E. Moore, *Ethics*, p. 162, and repeated in the paper "Nature of Moral Philosophy" in *Philosophical Studies*, New York, 1922. See also his paper "The Conception of Intrinsic Value" in *Philosophical Studies*. In the latter paper his definition of intrinsic value is value which "depends solely on the intrinsic nature of the thing in question." This is very similar to the definition discussed above, and is similarly dependent upon his general attitude toward value. It is not the purpose of his paper to develop a definition of intrinsic value, but from the definition given to show that intrinsic value cannot be "subjective." But it is obvious that it would never occur to anyone to define intrinsic value as he does, nor could he so define it unless he already held the theory that value is "objective." Hence, the whole paper is a huge *petitio principii*.

[3] See *Principia Ethica.* Cambridge, 1922, p. 36. Or in the later paper on "The Conception of Intrinsic Value," intrinsic value is not a property but the function of a property (pp. 272 ff., *loc. cit.*). But as he admits that he is unable to understand the difference between it and a property, and how it is dependent upon intrinsic properties, the distinction need not detain us.

value is not wholly objective in this sense. Value is dependent not only upon objective conditions, but upon a relation between what is objective and what is subjective. Conditions both of an object and of a sensibility are necessary for the existence of value. If this is the case, it is evident that an object could have no kind of value, intrinsic or otherwise, if nothing else than this object existed. A sensibility also must exist.

The "internality" of intrinsic value consists in this: the evaluating factor must be contained wholly within the experience of the value itself. No part of the datum of the experience is extraneous or borrowed from something outside of or beyond that experience. The intensity and the polarity, to be specific, are dependent upon nothing outside of the immediate experience. This view is not dependent upon any particular doctrine of the general nature of value, but is what makes the difference between intrinsic and instrumental value in any doctrine. An intrinsic value is such that the evaluating factor is within the experience itself. An instrumental value is such that the evaluating factor lies outside the actual immediate experience.

All aesthetic value is intrinsic value. The aesthetic attitude has been defined as absorption in immediate perceptual experience. Nothing that is truly relevant to the value, then, can go outside the immediate perceptual experience. The aesthetic attitude excludes the consideration of ends or results; therefore the evaluating factor cannot lie in ends or results. Likewise the attitude excludes rational and intellectual considerations, and therefore the evaluating factor for aesthetic value must be a component of the aesthetic experience.

3.

The meaning of the term "pleasure." "Pleasure" is a word which has often been used in the history of philosophy in connection with questions of value. It has been used in a multitude of ways and with various shades of meaning. Often these meanings have been very vague and general. As this is the case, the term should not be used in any philosophic discussion unless it be pointed out exactly what it shall be taken to mean.

Because of the misuses which have been made of the term "pleasure," psychology prefers not to use it at all, but instead to use the term "pleasantness." What psychology wants is a term to denote a fundamental state of feeling. Classically, "pleasure" and "pain" have been used to name the affective tones of consciousness, but psychology has now found reason to think that "pain" should be used as the name of a definite sensation. This sensation seems to be traceable to the stimulation of a definite kind of nerve (or possibly of any kind of nerve under certain conditions). But it has not been possible to find a sensory equivalent for pleasure or displeasure. The affective tone is something in addition to the content of any mental state. Any sensation may be pleasant or unpleasant. Even the stimulation of a pain receptor may, under certain conditions, be pleasant. The affective state is something in addition to the original stimulation, and as "pain" is the name of an original stimulation, the terms "pleasure" and "pain" are no longer used to denote affective states. Pain is usually unpleasant. "Pleasantness" and "unpleasantness" are the names of the affective states.

These are clumsy terms, but it seems necessary in psychology to use them in order to avoid irrelevant historical connotations. It is not necessary to avoid them in the present discussion if it is clearly pointed out that the term "pleasure" is used as an exact synonym of "pleasantness" when it sounds better. However, the term "pain" will never be used except as the name of a sensation. This is fixed psychological terminology. For the general affective state which is the opposite of pleasantness, "unpleasantness" or "displeasure" will always be used.

Pleasantness and unpleasantness are relative to each other. There is no absolute difference between them. They are commonly held to approach each other with a neutral zone between, but this neutral zone is specious. If neither a positive nor a negative affective state is very intense, lack of attention leads one to suppose that whatever mental content there is is neutral. This cannot be the case, however, for any state is either less pleasant, more pleasant, or of the same pleasantness as any other state. Each state of consciousness has its own specific degree of pleasantness or unpleasantness relative to any other state. Pleasantness and unpleasantness would not be relative terms if this were not true.

4.

The nature of pleasantness and unpleasantness. The basis for every psychological state must be sought in physiological

conditions. The function of the organism is called "life."
The organism has built up a reaction against that which is destructive of its life, and the conscious sign of this is pain. Only
those organisms have survived which have been successful in
avoiding stimuli destructive of life, and the race has been per-
petuated only by these relatively successful individuals. The
actual organic conditions of the progenitors of the present individual are not components of the consciousness of this individual. The details of racial experience do not remain in memory. The present individual is aware of only the sign of the
experience, the pain.[4]

As has been stated above, pain is the name of a sensation.
The affective tone that accompanies pain is unpleasantness.
The underlying reason why a stimulus is painful may be that
it is the sort of thing which was damaging or destructive and
which the ancestors of the race tended to avoid. Of course,
the present individual is not aware of this fact, however. He
is not aware of the history of the race in his every act. He
avoids painful stimuli because they are unpleasant. Unpleasantness is that affective state of consciousness the conditions of
which tend to be avoided, not for any conscious ulterior reason,
but only for the sake of not being in that state. Pleasantness
is the antithesis of unpleasantness; hence it may be said that
pleasantness is that affective state of consciousness the conditions of which tend to be repeated or held or kept or continued
only for the sake of being in that state.

---

[4] This analysis is based on the work of W. B. Cannon, *Bodily Changes in Pain,
Hunger, Fear and Rage*, New York, 1915; and G. W. Crile, *Origin and Nature of
the Emotions*, Philadelphia, 1915, and *Man an Adaptive Mechanism*, New York,
1916. See also, Crile, "Phylogenetic Association in Relation to the Emotions,"
in the *Proceedings of the American Philosophical Society*, Vol. 51, p. 76 (1912).

If there is no nervous activity of the organism (that is, if there is no exchange of nervous energy in the cerebral cells) there is no consciousness. The function of the organism is life, and the affective state that accompanies this which it tends to keep or continue is pleasantness. This activity, life, in the higher stages involves the exchange of nervous energy in the cerebral cells, and this consciousness is pleasant. The more activity, the more life there is; hence the pleasure might be expected to be greater. When the activity becomes excessive or destructive, or has tended toward what is excessive or destructive in the history of the race, the pleasantness merges into unpleasantness.

If any free and unimpeded flow of energy is suddenly inhibited, this condition might also be expected to cause a feeling of unpleasantness, for it creates a nervous tension which is not a normal condition of the organism. When any new activity of the individual which does not carry with it a strong affective state becomes closely associated with something else that is either pleasant or unpleasant, it tends to become pleasant or unpleasant itself by the process of conditioning. All these factors build up very complex experiences of pleasantness and unpleasantness in an adult. Few of the pleasures and displeasures of adult life are immediate signs of the physiologial conditions described above. But they do, all of them, seem to be based upon such conditions, some more and some less remotely. Adult reactions are highly conditioned. It may be difficult in any given case to find the exact reason why a certain thing is pleasant or unpleasant, because the actual circumstances of the conditioning are difficult to discover, but the above account seems to give the best basis for the attempt to understand the pleasures and displeasures of complex experience.

5.

The experience of positive aesthetic value is always pleasant.
The fact that the experience of beauty is pleasant might be established inductively by an investigation of each particular case of the experience.   Such a procedure would not establish any universality in the principle, however, and besides, it would beg the question at issue unless we already knew what beauty is and could establish it without reference to pleasure.   It has been apparent to thinkers in the history of aesthetics that the experience of beauty is pleasurable, and quotations could be adduced in authority from Plato down to the present.   The principle is best established, however, by demonstrating that the intrinsic nature of positive aesthetic value entails pleasure.

In the *General Theory of Value,* R. B. Perry distinguishes between what he calls "progressive" and what he calls "recurrent" interests.[5]   The recurrent interest is not an interest in going on to something not experienced in the immediate present, but is an interest in continuing what is being experienced in the present.   Aesthetic value is based on a recurrent interest.[6] A perceptual appearance is grasped in the present.   The interest is in it.   It is not mediated.   It does not look toward the future except in so far as it wants to continue the present into the future.   Pleasure has been seen to be the affective accom-

---

[5] R. B. Perry, *General Theory of Value,* New York, 1926, p. 243.
[6] *Ibid,* p. 245.

paniment of the tendency to keep or continue; therefore pleasure will always accompany a recurrent interest. Positive aesthetic values are based on recurrent interests, and thus always will be pleasant.

Another way of saying the same thing is that unpleasantness tends to inhibit or destroy the aesthetic attitude. The aesthetic attitude is contemplative or absorbed; but unpleasantness is the affective sign of the tendency to avoid. Unpleasantness calls to practical activity—to avoidance. Absorption may be aesthetic, but avoidance can never be. A tendency to avoid is incompatible with the aesthetic attitude.

There is no other reason for maintaining the aesthetic attitude than that it is pleasant. The aesthetic attitude is not something which is forced upon the individual, but something which he assumes. And it is an attitude which is very generally assumed. There must be a reason for this, but the very definition of the attitude precludes going out of itself for the reason. The reason cannot be that the attitude is useful or produces desired results or consequences. All of these considerations are extraneous and irrelevant to it. The only reason for assuming the aesthetic attitude is that it is pleasant. By the same token, it is apparent that the spectator would never willingly come in contact with the subject matter of the aesthetic experience or seek it when this subject matter is presented in artificial forms, as in art, unless the aesthetic experience were pleasant. The fact that such stimulation is greatly sought is evidence of the fact that it is pleasant.

6.

Pleasure is the evaluating factor. Aesthetic value is a value of such nature that the only adequate evaluating factor for it is pleasure. It is an intrinsic and a recurrent value. Its intrinsic nature demands that the evaluating factor should be found within itself. Its recurrent nature demands that the evaluating factor be of such a kind that it expresses the tendency to repeat or continue itself. Pleasure fulfills both of these requirements. It is always a component of the aesthetic experience, and it is the affective state of consciousness which accompanies the tendency to keep or continue. That it is the only adequate evaluating factor is apparent from the fact that it is the only reason for maintaining the aesthetic attitude. As value is a function of interest, that which maintains the interest is essential in making the value what it is. Pleasure is the measure of the aesthetic interest; it is the condition of the given intensity of every experience of aesthetic value.

Pleasure is the evaluating factor for aesthetic value. The more pleasure, the more positive value; the less pleasure, the less value. As the pleasure merges into displeasure, the positive value merges into disvalue. In the history of aesthetics, the pleasure of the aesthetic experience has been variously called satisfaction, agreeableness, delight, and so forth. Any of these terms is suitable if it is used to denote the fundamental affective state. This pleasure is greater in proportion as the normal and unimpeded activity of the organism is greater.

The perceptual grasp of an object involves activity of the organism; thus even the most simple perceptual grasp is pleasant unless some ulterior reason intrudes to inhibit the pleasure. Of course, this pleasure may not be very intense. It may be so slight that it escapes attention. Such a term as "delight" would hardly be appropriate to denote such a slight degree of pleasure.

7.

Pleasure is neither disembodied nor necessarily reflective. It must be emphasized throughout that pleasure is not a disembodied state. The use of the proper psychological designation, pleasantness, calls attention to this fact. Pleasantness is always the feeling tone of the consciousness of some particular content. It is never something of which the subject is aware by itself. This is the reason for the discovery made long ago, and incorrectly held by some moralists to refute hedonism, that pleasure can never be attained by seeking it. It is not a mental content by itself, but always the affective tone of the consciousness of some other content.

When it is maintained that pleasure, or pleasantness, is the evaluating factor for aesthetic value, it is not denied that one may be undergoing the greatest pleasure without a self-conscious "liking" of the experience. The conscious realization of liking the experience may come after; or it may not come at all. Even if it never comes, that is not an indication that there was no pleasure in the experience. It indicates merely that the individual did not reflect on his reactions. While the experience is present, it is sufficient unto itself. The individual is absorbed, and the more deeply he is absorbed, the more the indication of intense pleasure. The value is an intrinsic value. The individual may get pleasure from reflecting on his own reactions, but this is something in addition to aesthetic value and is in no way necessary to the most intense experience of value. The only pleasure which is the evaluating factor for aesthetic value is the pleasure of the aesthetic attitude.

To call the aesthetic experience "pleasant" means merely that it involves bodily conditions and physiological activities which tend to prolong or repeat themselves, and not to be avoided. To like the experience or the stimulus of the experience is the later recognition by reflective consciousness of this fact. One can have pleasure without reflecting on it.

8.

Aesthetic values are not measured by their scope. R. B. Perry finds three measures for the comparison of values: intensity, preference, and inclusiveness.[7] It has been shown that the intensity of aesthetic values is rendered intelligible by reference to the evaluating factor, pleasure. The standard of preference is the standard of taste, so called, and will be considered in a later chapter. The standard of inclusiveness does not apply to aesthetic values, because aesthetic values are intrinsic and immediate.

---

[7] R. B. Perry, *General Theory of Value,* Chapters XX and XXI.

One value can be included within another either as instrumental to the other or as a subsidiary part of the other. The first consideration does not apply to aesthetics, because no aesthetic values are instrumental. The second might be held to apply in the sense that a small design may be included within a larger design, or a chord in music is included within the whole composition, or a cloud within a sunset. To suppose this would be to forget that aesthetic value is to be found in perceptual grasp, and, as was brought out in Chapter IV, this grasp is an immediate unity. The value is to be found in the object perceived as a whole: it is in the whole, not in the parts. Therefore one cannot speak of any aesthetic value being a summation of lesser values. If a larger design is made up of smaller designs, the value of the whole is by no means the sum of the values of the parts. Any one part might have very little value, or even a negative value, if it were considered by itself. One chord in a composition might be very displeasing if it were by itself. The point is that it is not by itself. The whole composition is an aesthetic unity.

The only way to tell whether a part has aesthetic value by itself is to perceive it by itself and not in relation to the whole of which it is a part. If the perceptual grasp yields pleasure, then the part has value. In this case, however, it is no longer a part. It is, of itself, a new and different whole. Every aesthetic value is a unity. It is valuable for itself alone. Two whites are not whiter than one white, and similarly, two values are not more valuable than one value by virtue of their being two. For this reason aesthetic values are not ordered by their scope. If one cloud gives as much pleasure in contemplation as the whole sunset, then the whole sunset adds nothing, although it is larger. If one chord gives as much pleasure as the whole composition, then the rest of the composition is superfluous. Because of the slight amount of physiological activity involved in its apprehension, it may be doubted that the single cloud or the single chord can give as much pleasure; but even if this be the case it does not refute the point at issue. If the single cloud or chord *does* give as much pleasure, then it has as great a value. The poem of a few lines may be as beautiful as the poem of great length, and the novel of great scope is not a finer work of art merely because of its inclusiveness. Each thing is aesthetically valuable only for itself, and therefore in that respect stands alone. Its scope relative to other things is not a measure of its value.

CHAPTER VI

Aesthetic Value

1.

The nature of value in general. Value is a relational property of an object. Any kind of object whatever that comes before a mind may have value. The object *is not* the value; it *has* the value. The value is a property, but not a real property. That is, it is not a property essential to the existence of the object itself, nor is it a property that the object possesses independent of the relations into which it may come and unaltered by them. Value is a property attributed to an object by virtue of a relationship with a sensibility into which that object may come. The relation may be called taking interest in the object or exhibiting a specific attitude toward it. When such an interest is taken in an object, value is being experienced.

Value and the experience of value are not the same. It cannot be said without qualification that value is dependent upon the existence of an interest at any given time; that is, value is not temporally dependent upon a particular, existing interest. Value is a *property* attributed to an object, and is not dependent upon being appreciated. Value is in the object to be appreciated, and any individual may appreciate or fail to appreciate it. It is in the object only by virtue of the fact that the object may come into the specific relation, called "interest," with a sensibility. It is attributed to the object by virtue of this possibility. When the object enters into this relation with a sensibility at some particular time, then the value is actual. It is being appreciated or experienced. If it is not being appreciated or experienced, it is potential. Value is not the same as being valued, but an object has value only by virtue of the possibility of its being valued. When this possibility is unrealized, the value is potential. When it is realized, the value becomes actual; then only is there the experience or appreciation of value.

The only adequate criterion of potential value, however, is its realization. The potentiality is hypothetical. This is the reason for errors in judgments of value. Many writers seem to hold that the possibility of error in value judgment indicates that value is "objective" (that is, either a real property or the function of a real property of an object).[1] But a possibility of error is present in all judgments of value in case value is a relational property. If there is an actual existing relation between an object and a sensibility, the relational property is immediate and experienced. In this case there is no possibility of error; but if the relation is not an actuality, the attribution of the relational property can be only mediate—by means of

---

[1] This appears to me to be the case in the writings both of G. E. Moore, and of John Laird.

a judgment. The attribution depends upon the judged possibility that there might be such a relation; and this may or may not be the case.[2]

If the only adequate criterion of potential value is its realization, it is apparent that studies of value such as the present one should take their point of departure from the actual value (that is, from the value as experienced), and develop the conception of potential value only when it becomes necessary. Thus, in the present study, aesthetic value was first approached through the actual experience, when the aesthetic attitude is taken toward an object. Later it will become necessary to speak of aesthetic values which are not appreciated.[3]

Such values are potential. But there is no more confusion involved in calling an object "valuable" when the value is attributed to it only in the light of a possibility, than there is in calling bread "nourishing" when it is on the table. Obviously, at that time the bread is nourishing nothing. It is nutritive by virtue of the fact that it may be assimilated under certain conditions. That bread is nourishing is not a real property of the bread, but a relational property; and yet in involves no confusion to call bread nourishing.

2.

The nature of aesthetic value. Aesthetic value is value experienced in the perceptual aspects of phenomena. It arises from interest in these aspects regarded not as the sign of mean-

---

[2] Errors in judgments of instrumental values are·quite another matter. I am speaking above only of intrinsic values.

[3] Especially in the chapters on Taste and on Art.

ing or of fact, but only in their own nature. The value is actual when the object is being apprehended with pleasure or displeasure; otherwise it is potential. Thus, aesthetic value, in the broadest sense, is a property attributed to an object by virtue of the fact that it may be perceptually apprehended with pleasure or displeasure. If it is apprehended with pleasure, the value is positive; if with displeasure, the value is negative. If it is apprehended with more pleasure, the positive value is more intense; if with less pleasure, the value is less intense. If it is apprehended with great displeasure, the disvalue is intense; if with less displeasure, the disvalue is less intense. At the time the interest is directed toward the object, the value is actual. If the interest is not being exhibited, but is judged to be possible, the value is potential.

Thus, it may be said in a metaphor that positive aesthetic value is pleasure subject to the conditions of the aesthetic attitude; or that aesthetic value is pleasure in perceptual grasp. Such statements are only metaphors, however, for the value is not to be identified with the pleasure at all. The pleasure is not the value, it is the measure of the value—it is the evaluating factor.[4] A more precise statement would be that an

---

[4] To identify value with its evaluating factor is to commit what G. E. Moore calls the "naturalistic fallacy." See *Principia Ethica*, Cambridge, 1922, pp. 9–21. Holding this to be a fallacy is one of the few points upon which the present writer can agree with Moore's theory of value. To say, however, that the pleasantness of the experience of aesthetic value is the effective measure of the intensity of the value, is very different from saying that beauty is pleasure. Santayana commits the "naturalistic fallacy" if he intends his definition, "Beauty is pleasure regarded as the quality of a thing" (p. 49, *The Sense of Beauty*) to be taken literally. But his literal, technical definition is given in the previous sentence, "beauty . . . is value positive, intrinsic, and objectified." In the light of this, I think it better not to stress the less technical definition, but to regard it as a metaphor.

object has aesthetic value when pleasure is taken in its perceptual grasp. Any object which has perceptual aspects the apprehension of which is pleasant to any individual has positive aesthetic value for that individual.

3.

Perceptual grasp and aesthetic value. To begin with, simple perceptual grasp will bring about the conditions of pleasure unless something ulterior inhibits. Certainly, simple perceptual grasp is not what most persons are accustomed to call the experience of beauty. The present study does not imply that it is or that it should be. But perceptual grasp is the fundamental aesthetic experience, and is the basis for all aesthetic value. There is a possible scale of positive values ranging from the less to the more intense, and in the case of aesthetic values this scale starts with simple perceptual grasp. At the top may be some kind of rapture, but as long as the value is aesthetic, the perceptual grasp runs throughout the scale. The values that most persons call "characteristic" are probably along in the middle. Most ascend to the heights of rapture but seldom, and the simple perceptual grasp is not thought characteristic because the intensity of the value apprehended is so slight. Despite the fact that it may not be regarded as characteristic, it is fundamental.

If simple perceptual grasp is not an experience of aesthetic value (even though it is not very intense), exactly where in the scale above it does the value begin? The perceptual grasp is itself the result of an attitude (or interest) of the organism. The satisfaction of the interest may not give rise to a great degree of pleasure, and in consequence the value may be slight. But as Professor Perry succinctly says, "To assert that value begins at a certain level of value is as though one were to say that temperature begins at the freezing point or at the boiling point." [5]

As the object grows more complex, its grasp in perception involves more activity, and the conditions of interest and pleasure are increased. As the object grows complex, it also gets beyond perceptual grasp unless the parts are given in those structural and qualitative relationships which are the basis of aesthetic form. Thus the principles of form, such as pattern, rhythm, balance, proportion, the qualitative considerations which enter into harmony, and so on, are productive of more pleasure in perceptual experience, and are possessed of a greater degree of aesthetic value. In the apprehension of very simple rhythms, there may not be much activity involved; in this case there would not be great intensity of pleasure and the aesthetic value would be slight. In the apprehension of more complex and varied situations, more activity is involved, there is more pleasure, and consequently a higher degree of aesthetic value. If the situation is so complex that perception cannot grasp it—if the powers of perception are under a strain and still do not cope adequately with the situation—then the pleasure tends to merge into displeasure, and the positive value into disvalue.

---

[5] *General Theory of Value*, p. 596.

4.

Empathy and aesthetic value. If the perceptual apprehension of a situation is empathetic, the conditions of physiological activity, and hence of pleasure or displeasure, are greatly increased. Empathy almost always accompanies the apprehension of rhythms and balance. Empathy is the tendency to regard kinaesthetic reactions and incipient reactions that are a part of the observer's bodily condition as if they were perceptual aspects of the object.[6] Thus we speak of the rising mountain and undulating lines. The mountain, however, manifestly does not rise. It remains unmoving. It is our eyes and heads that are raised. And the lines do not undulate. We have the incipient imagery of an undulating motion when we see the lines. These kinaesthetic reactions, actual and incipient, are objectified into that which is perceived. Some supporters of the theory of empathy maintain that there is no perception except by the bodily and motor realization of the given situation.[7] That is, they maintain that perception itself is empathetic. Whether or not this is true, when perception is accompanied by empathy, the physiological activity of the organism is increased.

---

[6] The term "empathy" was invented to translate the German *Einfühlung*. There may be a question as to just what Lipps meant by *Einfühlung*. He probably did not mean only kinaesthetic empathy. See E. F. Carritt, *The Theory of Beauty*, London, 1923, Chapter XI. I am referring only to kinaesthetic empathy in the above.

[7] See Vernon Lee (Paget), *The Beautiful*, Cambridge, 1913, Chapters V and IX.

Empathy is a bodily and muscular readiness to act; often it is the actual beginning of an indicated action. This physiological activity is probably in addition to the activities of perception. It cannot be distinguished from perception except by intellectual analysis, because the bodily condition is objectified into, or "felt into," the perceptions; hence the distinction is irrelevant in the aesthetic attitude. The empathetic activity is absorbed into the perceptual activities in the aesthetic attitude. Thus the degree of pleasure in such an attitude may be greatly increased; and this enhances any aesthetic value apprehended.

Empathy may also increase the unpleasantness of the perception of any given situation. When the perceptual grasp of an object is not complete, there may be inhibited or frustrated or partial empathy. This is the case when a pictorial composition is "out of balance." There is a "run-down feeling"—a lack of equilibrium—which may be very unpleasant. Other examples of such an empathetic unpleasantness are unresolved dissonances in music, or a vocal note slightly out of tune. The bodily activity in this case is inhibited or frustrated, or else the activity involves a strain, and as has been pointed out, these conditions are conditions of unpleasantness. The complete and stable empathetic response increases the conditions of pleasure in the aesthetic attitude, and consequently increases the aesthetic value. The incomplete and unstable empathetic response increases the conditions of unpleasantness, and hence decreases the aesthetic value or increases the disvalue.

5.

Sense pleasure and aesthetic value. The pleasure taken in the perception of any object also may be greatly influenced by the sensuous agreeableness or disagreeableness of the content of perception. As sensation and sensuous pleasure are not definitive of the aesthetic experience, the sensuous content of aesthetic perception need not necessarily be agreeable, but as a matter of fact, if the sensuous content is agreeable, the total pleasure in the aesthetic attitude is increased; hence perceptions which are made up of agreeable sensuous material are likely to have greater value than those which are made up of disagreeable material.[8] It must be emphasized, however, that this dictum is merely a description of the greater value of a situation which is sensuously agreeable *if other things are equal.* Other things may never be equal; therefore nothing *a priori* can be said concerning the value of any particular situation just because it is or is not sensuously agreeable.

Sensations, except as they are the content of perceptions, are not the substance of aesthetic values, hence the gratification of appetite is never an aesthetic pleasure nor is it an experience of aesthetic value. The gratification of appetite is not pleasure in perceptual grasp. The pleasure of the gratification of appetite is dependent upon specific physiological conditions which have little or nothing to do with the processes of perception or with

---

[8] See above, Chapter III, Section 7.

the aesthetic attitude. These conditions are completely internal, and when there is any consciousness of them they are recognized to be internal and are more or less unpleasant. During the process of removing this unpleasantness, pleasure will result. This pleasure is not the pleasure of the aesthetic attitude. It is not pleasure in the perceptual grasp of an appearance. The pleasure of the gratification of an appetite quickly passes over into satiety when the physiological conditions of the appetite are removed. Aesthetic pleasure, however, as it is not dependent upon the removal of some unpleasant physiological condition, does not pass over into satiety, and is not lessened in proportion as it is gratified. If one grows tired of the aesthetic experience and wants to leave it, he does so because of the breakdown of attention and not because of satiety.

The observation of this fact that there seems to be a permanence in aesthetic pleasure which does not belong to other pleasures has led some writers to hold that the differentia of the aesthetic lies in permanence of pleasure. H. R. Marshall says, "Those pleasures are judged to be aesthetic which (relatively speaking) are permanently pleasurable in memory." [9] This may be true, but if so, is true for the reason given above. It is not an adequate criterion until after the pleasure is remembered. And more important, if any pleasure which had little to do with perception should, for any reason at all, and after the fact, become permanently pleasurable in memory, that would not make it aesthetic. Many moral pleasures would fall under this definition. The apparent permanence of aesthetic

---

[9] H. R. Marshall, *Pain, Pleasure and Aesthetics*, London, 1894, p. 110.

pleasures is not a criterion whereby they can be distinguished from other pleasures. The permanence is due to the fact that aesthetic pleasures are not based on the gratification of appetite.

6.

Emotion and aesthetic value. It has been brought out above that emotion is not definitive of the aesthetic experience, but neither is it irrelevant to aesthetic value.[10] When the emotions are aroused, the physiological activity of the organism is increased, and thus the conditions of pleasure are influenced. Aesthetic perception may arouse emotion, and if these emotions are agreeable, the pleasure of the experience is increased. But again it is necessary to emphasize that this principle in no way demands that the aesthetic experience should be emotional, or that the emotionality present be an evaluating factor for the intensity of the value. The emotion is a factor which is not essential, but, if other things are equal, a pleasant emotion increases the value. Other things may not be equal, however, as in some types of romantic music in which a highly emotional appeal is combined with a flimsy formal structure.

The actual sources of pleasure in any particular experience of aesthetic value are often determined by the standard of taste of the individual. The factors which have been brought out in Sections 3 to 6 of the present chapter operate to increase the intensity of aesthetic values without respect to the individual.

---

[10] See above, Chapter III, Section 8.

In addition to them there are many individual factors operating. It may be that a person is accustomed to certain things, and strange things do not excite his interest. He takes no pleasure in them, perhaps only because he does not pay sufficient attention to them. The actual reasons why any particular perception is pleasant or unpleasant are very complex, and perhaps never can be completely known in any concrete instance because all the circumstances of conditioning in the past history of the individual can never be known. Factors such as those mentioned above are operative without respect to the individual. The questions of taste will be considered in a later chapter.

7.

Beauty and aesthetic value. The word *beauty*, when used by most persons in ordinary speech, is probably intended to mean a relatively great degree of positive aesthetic value when this value is exhibited in objects possessing more or less traditional forms of harmony and proportion. It seems to be assumed also that there must be at least a minimum of sensuous charm in the beautiful object. In most writings on aesthetics, however, "beauty" has been taken to mean the whole of aesthetic value. Even in this case there is an ambiguity present, for some writers, such as Kant, have decided that the beautiful and the sublime must be carefully distinguished from each other, although each is a form of aesthetic value. Schopenhauer followed Kant here. Croce deplores the tendency to view these and like differences as of fundamental importance in aesthetics,[11] and Carritt follows him in this,[12] but even Carritt finally thinks that it is necessary to distinguish between the beautiful and the ludicrous.[13] This is after he has defined aesthetics in terms of beauty,[14] and yet he seems to think that the ludicrous is or may be aesthetic.[15]

It is not conducive to clear thinking to make beauty synonymous with positive aesthetic value. The common conception of beauty is vague. Where the common meaning was referred to in the preceding paragraph, the words "relatively great," "more or less," and "at least a minimum" were used, because the meaning is vague. And it will always remain vague because "beauty" is a word rich in poetic and literary connotations. Furthermore, it is preferable that it remain so. If it be carefully defined as a clear and definite term, and used in this way always, the writer who so uses it lays himself open to misunderstandings, because the literary term is deeply ingrained in his readers, who find it difficult to keep in mind that the word does not mean the same to him as it does to them. More dangerous than this, however, is the fact that even after the term has been shorn of its rich and vague connotations, these connotations almost inevitably creep back into the use of the term by the writer himself. Even the writer who defines beauty to be synonymous with aesthetic value hesitates to call

---

[11] B. Croce, *Aesthetic,* trans. by Ainslie, London, 1922, Chapter XII.
[12] E. F. Carritt, *The Theory of Beauty,* London, 1923, pp. 204 ff.
[13] Ibid., Appendix A.
[14] Ibid., pp. 2–3.
[15] Ibid., p. 307.

the grotesque or the merely pretty, "beautiful." If he does so he feels constrained to explain himself and perchance to apologize.[16]

Hence, it is inadequate to define aesthetics as the philosophy of beauty. Most persons would hesitate to apply the term "beauty" to lesser degrees of aesthetic value, but these lesser degrees cannot be disregarded. The term "beauty" cannot be applied to the disvalue; yet the consideration of the disvalue cannot be omitted. The term "beauty" is best used to denote only a part of the general field of aesthetic value, and that part need not be carefully delimited, but can be left more or less vague and only roughly defined by poetic and literary connotations. The philosophy of beauty is only a part of the field of aesthetics. Aesthetics is the philosophic study of perceptual intuition, or more narrowly, the study of the value that is to be found in the data of perceptual intuition. It is the philosophic study of aesthetic value.

One often finds another use of the term "beauty." Beauty is sometimes identified with the objective principles of aesthetic form, such as the traditional kinds of proportion, harmony, and balance. This is referred to as "Greek beauty" or "classic beauty." There is danger of confusion in this use of the term unless it is distinguished from aesthetic value, but those who

---

[16] The cases cited in the previous paragraph of distinctions between beauty and other conceptions of aesthetic value are evidence of this. An exactly contrary, but just as confusing, situation is developed by Croce, who insists that the "kinds" have no philosophical significance, but that there are no degrees of beauty, for beauty is perfect. (See Croce, *Aesthetic,* p. 79.) There are, however, degrees of ugliness. Therefore, it appears that most persons never or seldom experience beauty at all. They experience only degrees of ugliness. Such a standpoint is nothing but a verbal quibble introduced by trying to use an essentially poetic term with technical precision.

use the term in this way do not seem so to distinguish it. This tendency is increased by the fact that "ugliness" is often used to denote the absence of this "classic beauty," as when one speaks of a grotesque object as ugly. "Classic beauty," however, denotes certain objective principles of aesthetic form. If the term "beauty" is used in this sense, it must be distinguished from aesthetic value, because, as has been seen, the objective principles of aesthetic form are not value; they are only conditions of the existence of the value. To overstep this distinction in the use of the term "beauty" is only to exhibit confusion.

8.

Art, nature, and aesthetic value. Many doctrines define aesthetics as the philosophy of art, and find their subject matter in the appreciation of art or in the experience of the artist. Such doctrines hold either explicitly or implicitly that the only objects of real aesthetic value are objects of human contruction, that is, art. Questions relating especially to art will be considered in a later chapter. At present, the only question at issue is where aesthetic value can be found. Nature is often excluded or disregarded in the study of aesthetics.[17] Can aesthetic value be found in nature or can it not? The present study took its point of departure not from metaphysical assumptions or artistic prejudices, but from reflection upon a vague and undefined, yet characteristic experience which most per-

---

[17] For example, Hegel excluded nature. This tendency is also widely prevalent among contemporary writers. Clive Bell is an example.

sons seem to have at times. They suppose that they have this experience in contact with natural objects. Has any reason been found to indicate this assumption erroneous?

Aesthetic value has been found to inhere in the perceptual aspects of phenomena, and there are perceptual aspects in natural objects as well as in objects of art. If there is pleasure in the perceptual grasp of these natural objects, then they have aesthetic value, and nature as well as art can be possessed of aesthetic value. Perhaps the pleasure in the perception of natural objects is not as great as that excited by works of art, but to exclude the consideration of nature for this reason is not justifiable. Any object which has perceptual aspects the apprehension of which is pleasurable has aesthetic value. Nothing having perceptual aspects can be arbitrarily excluded.

CHAPTER VII

Derived Aesthetic Value

1.

Santayana's theory of the expressiveness of the aesthetic object. The aesthetic values that have been described up to this point in the present theory have been in large measure material and formal values. That is, if one adopts the division which Santayana makes of beauties into material, formal, and expressive, little foundation has been given for expressive beauty. The material and the formal cannot be separated except in abstraction, but either one may receive greater emphasis than the other in any experience. Expressiveness differs from these two, according to Santayana, in its origin. Any object becomes expressive through the associations it has acquired in past experience.[1] If these associations act in such a way as to

---

throw a penumbra of pleasure about the object without taking
the attention away from the object or diverting the aesthetic
attitude, there is expressive beauty. Santayana points out explicitly and with emphasis that associations remembered in
addition to the object are not part of the expressive beauty of
the object. The associations must be absorbed into the object
and appear to be a part of it.

2.

*Expressiveness depends on the nonaesthetic aspects of the
object.* The apparent absorption of associations into the aspect
of a perceived object is possible because perception itself takes
place in the light of the past experience of the organism. The
aesthetic experience is not sundered from the rest of experience,
and if the present study has seemed to speak of it as if it were,
that has been for the sake of analytic clarity. It is not true
that the aesthetic aspects of an object have nothing to do with
other aspects, and that aesthetic value is dependent on these
alone, uninfluenced by anything else. The aesthetic experience
is not something absolutely pure in this sense. It is probable
that nothing in existence is absolutely pure. Purity itself is
an analytic abstraction, and does not seem to exist in the
empirical world.

Aesthetic objects are not things which are, in some mysteri-
ous way, different from the things of ordinary experience. The
aesthetic aspects of any object do not set it apart from mundane
experience, for the aesthetic aspects are the perceptual aspects,

and mundane experience is perceptual before it is anything else. The aesthetic experience is not an esoteric affair which in some ineffable way is on a plane of spirituality sundered from that of ordinary life. The aesthetic is the very foundation of all human experience, and aesthetic value is not extraneous to the other values of life, nor are they irrelevant to it.

The connections which exist between the aesthetic and other experiences raise a problem that has been very awkward for the history of aesthetics. In the consideration of this problem, more errors have crept into aesthetic theory than in any other way. All objects of the aesthetic experience have, in addition to the aesthetic, nonaesthetic aspects. Can these nonaesthetic aspects have any bearing on the aesthetic experience? Can they influence in any way the aesthetic value of the object? Is poetry which teaches a lesson more or less beautiful because of the lesson? Can a painting which conveys scientific information, or music used to excite a martial spirit, be beautiful? Since the problem is concerned with the nonaesthetic aspects of the object, it offers a wide entrance for nonaesthetic considerations into aesthetic theory.

There may be such a thing as "pure beauty," whatever that is supposed to mean. In the terminology of the present study, it would mean that an object would have positive value if regarded in the aesthetic attitude, but would have no value if regarded from the point of view of any other attitude. It is doubtful that such could ever be the case for the reason given above, that purity itself is an analytic abstraction. If there is any such thing as pure beauty in this sense, it is certain that it does not enter into experience very often. Every object which enters into experience seems to have many different aspects. This means that many different attitudes can be taken toward it. Most objects of the aesthetic experience are of this kind. Is there any relation between the nonaesthetic aspects and the aesthetic? Can the one influence the other in any way? Can the aesthetic value be affected by aspects of the object which are nonaesthetic?

It has been found that the essence of the aesthetic experience is perceptual grasp. Aesthetic value is dependent upon perceptual grasp. Nevertheless, the objects which have aesthetic value also have nonaesthetic aspects. The problem resolves itself, then, into the question, can the various nonaesthetic aspects of an object influence the perception of that object? If they do, how do they? If it can be found that they influence perception, it will have to be asserted that they are not always irrelevant to aesthetic value. If it can be discovered *how* they influence perception, it will be easy to discover in just what way they affect aesthetic value.

3.

Nonaesthetic aspects of an object influence the perception of the object. To say that any given object has many different aspects means that it can be regarded from the point of view of different attitudes. A tree may be regarded as beautiful; or it may be regarded as worth so much money; or as containing so many board feet of lumber; or as the thing under which one played when a boy; or as a visible sign of history, as under its branches, perhaps, some important event, long past, was consummated. Each of these aspects denotes a different attitude in the observer of the tree. Is the tree a beautiful thing, is it an economic thing, is it a practical thing, a sentimental thing, or an historic thing in its own nature? If it is any one of these, it is all. To say that it is predominantly one or the other is merely to say that one attitude or another is the attitude usually taken toward it.

Any phenomenon is predominantly aesthetic or moral or intellectual in case the habitual attitude of the observer toward it is aesthetic or moral or intellectual. The same phenomenon which is predominantly of one kind at one time may be predominantly of another kind at some other time: the habitual attitude of the observer toward it may change. He may regard it in one way at one time and in another at some other time. Even though at one time the attitude may be predominantly or primarily of one kind, yet it is always possible to take some other attitude toward it: the other aspects of the object are potentially in it. Thus any object that seems primarily to be of one nature may secondarily be of other natures.

Any phenomenon which is primarily or predominantly intellectual or moral or practical has secondary aesthetic aspects. There is a perceptual aspect, or a possible perceptual aspect, even though it be only by symbolization, of everything. Even in case this perceptual aspect is only secondary (that is, is not being attended to or regarded in its own nature), it is entering into the whole experience, making it in part what it is. Any experience may be predominantly intellectual, but something is being perceived. The tree may be a problem in log scaling, but perceptual appearances are being intuited.

In like manner, phenomena which are primarily aesthetic have secondary intellectual and moral and practical and other aspects. The tree may be beautiful, but the number of board feet in it can be ascertained. It may be regarded primarily from the point of view of the aesthetic attitude, but there are other possible attitudes, and the aspects regarded in these other possible attitudes are not irrelevant to the way it is perceived. It is true that perceptions are ordinarily regarded as signs of facts or meanings, and that experience is predominantly aesthetic only when they are not so regarded, but are regarded in their own nature as perceptions. Even when the aesthetic attitude is taken and the experience is primarily aesthetic, the significance or meaning of the perceptions is still present. It is thrust into the background; it is only secondary; but it is real, even if it is not uppermost in attention.

If one knows trees thoroughly, as a forester, as a botanist, as a lumberman, and as a boy, he sees something very different when he looks at a tree than does one who has never had wide acquaintance with trees. This is true when he looks at the tree from the viewpoint of the aesthetic attitude, as well as when he looks at it from other viewpoints. The actual perceptual data before him are different, as imagery is part of the content of actual perception. In addition, his perceptual grasp is much more complete and adequate than is that of the observer with a narrow experience. More of the values potential in any given object are apprehended by the observer of wide experience.

4.

The nature of derived aesthetic value. Any value apprehended in the aesthetic attitude is an aesthetic value. Any value apprehended in the moral attitude is a moral value. The same is true of other attitudes and values, for value is a function of the attitude and of the object. All apprehension of value is dependent upon the predominant attitude of the individual. If the attitude changes, the kind of value apprehended likewise changes. If any object that is predominantly moral has secondary economic or aesthetic aspects, these aspects cannot give rise to the apprehension of economic or aesthetic value as long as they remain secondary. The predominant attitude is moral; hence, any value apprehended will be moral. In the same way, the secondary moral or economic aspects of an object predominantly aesthetic do not give rise to the apprehension of moral or economic value. The value apprehended in this attitude is aesthetic value; hence, if the secondary aspects influence the apprehension of value at all, it is by being absorbed into, or fused with, the aesthetic value. This is possible in so far as the secondary aspects influence the perceptual grasp of the situation.

The secondary aspects of any object that is predominantly aesthetic give rise to derived aesthetic values. Aesthetic value is dependent upon the perceptual grasp of an object, and the secondary aspects, at least in part, make that grasp what it is. If any kind of object has ever entered the intellectual or moral (or other) experience of the individual, the fact that it has so entered is always relevant to future perceptions of that kind of object. Even the intellectual or moral or other past experiences are relevant to present perception, for one perceives an object in the light of *all* his experience with that or similar objects. It has been pointed out that in the aesthetic attitude the perceptual imagination cannot be differentiated from "actual" perception,[2] and it can hardly be doubted that the perceptual imagination has as its objects only those things whose elements are taken from past experience. All and any past experience is relevant to the activities of the perceptual imagination, and therefore is relevant to any object of the aesthetic attitude.

These past experiences are necessarily not components in present consciousness. At the moment of perception, the individual is not aware of the whole body of past experience, even though these past experiences are factors in making the present perception what it is. He is not separately aware of the secondary aspects of the object, though they contribute to its perceptual grasp. The perception in its own nature is immediate. The aesthetic experience is unified. The secondary aspects of the object do not stand apart, and they are not attended to in their own nature. They would not be secondary if they were. As the actual perceptual grasp of the object may be influenced by, or in part derived from, the intellectual, moral, practical, and other secondary aspects of the object, and as aesthetic value is to be found in this perception, the

---

[2] See above, Chapter III, Section 6.

aesthetic value of the object may be influenced by, or in part derived from, these other aspects.

A direct aesthetic value is that value which is apprehended in the perceptual aspect of an object in so far as it is dependent upon the form and material of the object, and is independent of intellectual, moral, or other aspects which that object might have. The aesthetic value of a simple tone or a single color may be presumed to be almost wholly direct, and the value of an abstract line design would be, in a large measure, direct. A derived aesthetic value is that value which is apprehended in the perceptual aspect of an object in so far as it is influenced by intellectual, moral, practical, and other aspects of the object. In concrete experience, direct and derived values may never be found distinct and separate from each other. Theoretically, direct could exist without derived, but the derived, by very definition, could not exist without the direct.[3] The distinction is analytic and explanatory. In concrete perception, all is one. The aesthetic experience is immediate and unified. It is clear, however, that a landscape painting (or an actual landscape), if it has any aesthetic value, has a larger measure of derived value than has an abstract design, because a person of ordinary experience cannot see it except as a composition of known and recognized things, with possible intellectual and moral and sentimental associations. A poem has a still larger proportion of derived values, because the appreciation of the poem depends upon the meanings of the words and sentences making it up.

---

[3] This is the theoretic principle lying behind Santayana's insistence that "the value of the second term must be incorporated in the first." See p. 197, *Sense of Beauty.*

It might be conceived that the amount to which a secondary aspect can influence the perception of an object is slight and unimportant. The influence upon perception may be slight, but even so, it does not follow that it is unimportant. It may make the precise difference between adequate perceptual grasp and inadequate. In another case, without this influence, there might be no positive value at all. The secondary aspects may be what determine whether the object is perceived with pleasure or with displeasure. In other cases, the value might be weak and tenuous without these aspects, while with them it becomes rich. The difference between synthetic vanilla flavoring and the genuine extract is very slight, but the difference that makes the genuine so preferable lies in the presence of vegetable oils which are, chemically speaking, impurities.

5.

Failure to distinguish between direct and derived values generates theories of false emphasis. Without the distinction between direct and derived aesthetic values, the study of aesthetics is in a hopeless muddle when it considers how the apprehension of aesthetic value can be influenced by other experiences. Failure to make the distinction has led many thinkers to confuse aesthetic with other kinds of value. Hegel formulated an intellectualistic theory. For him, art is the presentation of Truth in sensuous form.[4] It is the perceptualization of the

---

[4] Hegel, *Philosophy of Fine Art*, Introduction, English translation by Bosanquet, London, 1905, p. 141.

concept. Art cannot be separated from its Idea, and, in the advance of dialectic, disappears into philosophy. It is only an imperfect kind of philosophy. This theory is the result, not of a clear-eyed view of the aesthetic experience, but of an obsession with his system and a lack of understanding of the relation between aesthetic value and the intellectual experience.

Ruskin and Tolstoy both tended to confuse aesthetic value with moral value because they did not see the way the one influences the other. Tolstoy's *What is Art?* [5] contains a large body of aesthetic theory, but it is so confused with moral questions that on a first reading of the book it often remains unnoticed. These men have seen that intellectual significance or moral approval or condemnation influences aesthetic appreciation; hence, they have tended to confuse aesthetic and non-aesthetic experience.

On the other hand, some thinkers have been so intent upon the direct values that they have overlooked the derived. Clive Bell maintains that representation in painting can never add anything to the aesthetic value of the painting. The representation is not structural or formal; hence, it is irrelevant to aesthetic value. [6] It is true that the judgment of fidelity of representation in painting is intellectual. Therefore there is no direct aesthetic value to be found in representation as such in painting, but the representation may be a source of derived value. It has been shown above that representation influences perceptual grasp. [7] The perception of any familiar object in-

---

[5] L. N. Tolstoy, *What is Art?* New York, 1898.

[6] Clive Bell, *Art*, London, 1914, pp. 25 and 58.

[7] See above, Chapter III, Section 4, and Chapter IV, Section 4.

cludes sense images which are not actually presented by physical stimulation. These come from past experience, and thus the intuition of the perceptual data is influenced by past experience. Both in this way, and in the fact that familiarity with an object facilitates the grouping of the elements which makes possible the grasp of a complex situation, the representation influences perception and therefore may be a source of derived aesthetic values.

6.

Illustration of derived aesthetic value taken from mathemathics. When a mathematician derives a complex formula that gratifies him, puts down the pencil, looks at the paper with admiration, and exclaims "Beautiful!," he may be undergoing a genuine aesthetic experience. His remark cannot be dismissed in a cursory manner as merely metaphorical. It is possible that it is not a metaphor. Perhaps another observer would not be tempted to call the thing beautiful, but the other would not see what the mathematician sees.

It is true that what the mathematician sees is a very complicated product of his knowledge and imagination. If the mathematician's experience is in even a remote degree aesthetic, he is concerned with perceptual data when he says "beautiful." It must be remembered that perception is not the same as sensation. The actual sensations he has may be presumed to be very similar to the sensations which any one else would have in looking at the paper. It might be said that they are sensations of black and white which are given by lines on a piece of paper, but of course this is already naming perceptions. He is not regarding these lines as a pattern or a design. He is regarding them in a way that is wholly foreign to the non-mathematical observer. There is a perceptual datum before him which is quite different from that before the other observer. Without doubt, the usual aspect of the lines and the greatest concern of the mathematician is intellectual. But there is the perceptual symbolization of a mathematical reality before him. For the moment, the meaning has completely merged with its concrete symbolization.[8] If, for the moment, he does not center his attention on the processes of proof and reason which are involved, or on the scientific or practical consequences of the formula, but contemplates it merely as an object to be contemplated, he is in the aesthetic attitude and is experiencing aesthetic value.

This is very largely a derived aesthetic value, because the perceptual data which is before the mathematician depends for its very nature upon intellectual significance (which gives rise, perhaps, to dramatic imagination). The datum before him is not before the other observer, for the significance is not present to the other observer. The slight degree of direct aesthetic value in this experience is of very little intensity. It is to be presumed that the direct value would be somewhat similar to the mathematician and to the other observer, for the object in its actual structure is the same, and the sense organs of the two individuals may be presumed to be similar. Each of the two observers perceives the lines on the paper, but the pleasure

---

[8] If this were not possible, poetry could not possess much aesthetic value.

involved in such perception is probably not very intense. In this example, the greatest source of pleasure lies in the secondary aspects of the object. In objects which are ordinarily called beautiful, the larger proportion of the value is direct. Even here it may be that, as was brought out above, the derived is of importance out of all proportion to its size.

7.

The influence of cognition on appreciation, illustrated from music. Is there a cognitive element in the aesthetic experience? This question is often asked, but it never ought to be asked, at least not in this form, for the answer to it depends on what it means, and as it stands it is highly ambiguous. Questions asked in philosophy must be clear, and this is far from clear. Is there a cognitive element in perception? No and yes. This still is not a clear question. If it is supposed to mean that, in actual "thick experience," concepts can be found, then certainly, there is always a cognitive element in perception. Concepts are known only as they are analyzed out of actual experience.

If, however, the question means to ask whether perception is a cognitive act, then of course the answer is "No." Perceptual intuition, in its own nature, is not cognitive. If the percepts are taken as symbols of fact, they have a cognitive or intellectual value; and this is all that percepts are valued for outside the aesthetic experience. Perception in its own nature is immediate apprehension. It *seems* to be given. By analysis, cognitive elements can be found in it, but they are not apparent upon the face of it. When a perception is regarded as a significant symbol, cognitive value is being discovered in it. When it is regarded merely as it appears to be, aesthetic value is being discovered.

Is there a cognitive element in the aesthetic experience? No, not if this means that the aesthetic experience is cognitive; but yes, if it means that cognition or knowledge can affect the aesthetic experience. Cognition can influence the aesthetic experience in an indirect way. The conception of derived values is the explication of the way in which it does so. It enters into the aesthetic experience as it affects perception. The "fact" in the perception of fact influences the perceptual intuition. The basis for this has been stated. In no other way than as they affect perception can cognitive elements enter into the *aesthetic* experience. If they enter in any other way, the experience is no longer predominantly aesthetic.

A good illustration of the way that cognitive elements can affect the aesthetic experience and give rise to derived aesthetic values may be found in musical appreciation. This illustration is taken because music is probably the purest of all the arts; that is, the values to be apprehended are to a large extent direct values; thus it is especially instructive to see how the derived values dependent upon cognition affect this experience. Music is a highly complex medium. In music, many sounds of different pitch and quality are given at the same time, and the temporal pattern may be long. In a symphony, often there are dozens of different tones of different pitch and timbre at the same time, and the whole sometimes extends over the greater part of an hour.   This is a high degree of complexity.

The ordinary appreciation of music is rather primitive, and the pleasure is confined largely to the sensuous agreeableness of the tones and harmonies put into rhythmic patterns.   If one has a technical knowledge of the structure and form of music, however, what he actually perceives is far beyond what it is possible for the common man to perceive.   He is thoroughly acquainted with the possibilities of the situation.   He is accustomed to its complexity.   He knows what the composer and the performers are trying to do.   He has tried to do it himself; hence it is second nature with him, and it takes no effort of attention to grasp it.   All his knowledge is in the background; it is secondary.   If the appreciation is truly aesthetic, the knowledge is never explicit.   The hearer is listening to the music.   He is not primarily thinking of technique and performance, but his knowledge of technique and performance makes it possible for him to hear what he hears; it makes his perceptual grasp more adequate.   The knowledge gives rise to derived aesthetic values, but the experience of one who knows music is primarily intellectual no more than is that of the common man.   He is perceiving form to which the common man is blind.   He hears what the common man does not hear.   It would be a travesty to ask many habitual concertgoers whether they appreciated Bach or Beethoven, since they never heard the music Bach or Beethoven really wrote.   What many auditors hear is a more or less vague blur of sound, or at least, only a melody against a vaguely heard background.   Although this be very pleasant, it is not the music Bach or Beethoven or even Johann Strauss composed.

8.

Aesthetic expressiveness is dependent upon derived values. The aesthetic expressiveness of an object depends upon derived aesthetic values. When one has had much experience with objects of a certain kind, past associations become fused with the present presentation of such an object. These associations give rise to secondary aspects. One sees the object in a way in which he would not if it were not for them, and the object becomes expressive. They may be chance associations and utterly fortuitous, they may be imaginary and romantic, or they may be logical and rational: it matters no whit; their expressiveness operates in the aesthetic experience in the same way. If the associations are such that the present object is perceived with added pleasure, they yield derived aesthetic values, and if these are intense enough, they may be called expressive beauty. Intuited data, as such, have value. They also stir the associative imagination. This is the basis for all expressive beauty.[9]

One may enjoy a scene because it is the kind of scene in which he spent the happiest days of his youth. Whenever he

---

[9] It is apparent that I am using the term "expression" in the way in which Santayana defines it, not in the way in which it is used by Croce, by Bosanquet (*Three Lectures on Aesthetic,* London, 1915) and a host of others. See Santayana's *Sense of Beauty,* Part IV, for his treatment of the subject. See also Prall, *Aesthetic Judgment,* Chapters X–XIII, for a full treatment from Santayana's viewpoint.

looks at similar scenes, all the pleasures of the former happy days are recalled. Such pleasure is not aesthetic because it is not pleasure in the perceptual grasp of the present object. The pleasure is taken not so much in the present scene as in the memories of the past. If, on this account, one likes the present scene, the liking is sentimental. When the scene leads away from itself to associations and memories, the observer is not in the aesthetic attitude; he does not contemplate the perceptual aspect before him, but is engrossed in memories—memories which are only suggested by what is before him. If, however, one does not remember explicitly the scenes of the past and maintains the aesthetic attitude toward the present scene, the pleasure is drawn into the evaluating factor for the aesthetic value and becomes a part of it. Then the scene has expressive beauty. The associations yield derived aesthetic values. This is what Santayana means when he says that in case our pleasure in a scene is not aesthetic, "a little dimming of our memory will often make it so." [10]   Much natural beauty is expressive in this way.

There is also another kind of expressiveness in natural beauty. Trees show sturdiness and rocks strength. Storms are full of terror and yawning chasms are awful. These and like metaphors are given their force by a real expressiveness of the object: they are precipitates of derived aesthetic values. If we had not seen trees stand against the wind and overcome the cold, they would not express sturdiness. Their resistance seizes our imagination and they come at last to appear to be just the right sort of thing to rebuff the onslaughts of the weather. They

---

[10] *Sense of Beauty*, p. 194.

symbolize sturdiness. If we had never been aroused to terror by a storm, it would not be terrible; but it arouses our terror so inevitably that at last it seems to be full of the very elements of terror itself.

Expressiveness of this sort is akin to another kind, which is often known as "functional beauty." The airplane of today is a very much more beautiful thing than was that of 1910. Part of the reason for this is direct: that is, the added aesthetic value is a direct value to be found in the economy of line and proportion. These are formal properties. In addition to them, there is much added beauty in the airplane of today because it appears to be a thing made to fly, designed well to perform its function. There are two reasons for this beauty of function, both of which are based on past experience and associations. In the first place, we have now seen many airplanes of the present design fly, but airplanes were a rare sight in 1910. In the second place (and probably more important), the airplane of today looks much more like a bird than did the old models.

The beauty of function arises from the expressiveness of an object. It is a derived aesthetic value, dependent upon our knowledge that the object performs its function well and reinforced by the dramatic imaginations which may surround it because of mystery, or of likeness to natural objects, or because through long acquaintance it seems to embody emotions which it inspires in us. None of these factors would be enough to give it beauty without a formal basis. For example, the common wood telephone pole with many crossbars performs its function of supporting wires admirably and simply. Nevertheless, even a long acquaintance with this performance does not make telephone poles things of beauty. Beside a powerful steam locomotive, an electric locomotive much more efficient and functionally perfect looks like a monstrous cheese box on wheels, and part of the reason for the "functional beauty" of the steam locomotive is that it spits fire and fury, while for its power the electric locomotive depends on a thin line overhead.

An illustration of many of the different kinds of expressiveness may be found in the human body. Of course, the beauty of the body is to a large extent formal. Occasionally bodies may be found of exquisite grace of line, perfection of proportion, and delicacy of texture. In addition to this, *we* are bodies, and know how it is to be a body. Limbs, fingers, features, all have functions to fulfill, and we know intimately the forms which help and those which hinder these functions. The human body is a natural object [11] and one with which we are passing well acquainted. If birds seem fitted to fly, how much more do human bodies seem fitted to carry on their varied activities. If storms are full of terror, how much more is it true that bodies may express anger or love. And in addition to all this, if man were and always had been a sexless creature, would the beauty of the body be the same to him as it is now? Manifestly no, for part of its expressive beauty is derived from associations and conditions which are biological, not aesthetic.

Works of art may be expressive in many different ways accordingly as different kinds of past associations and knowledge give rise to derived aesthetic values. They may express the

---

[11] This is a point that many of those who argue against the beauty of nature seem to forget. To say that the body is an expression of the spirit serves only in a very incomplete way to set it off from other natural objects.

nature of the medium.   An immense gothic cathedral built of brick is not as beautiful as if built of stone, and one of the reasons for this is that we know bricks crumble.   Or works of art may express the purposes, interests, and personality of the artist.   This is true, however, only in case we know something about the artist or construct some story about him in our imagination.   Much of van Gogh's painting is mad.   Fortunately for the story, we know that van Gogh was mad.   If we did not, we would reason out that he must have been mad. Or if we knew that he was not mad, we would invent some story about the sublimation of a perfectly repressed madness. It is evident that the madness expressed in the painting is dependent upon our knowledge of the case, or upon association of the case with others more or less similar to it.

That an object or situation is considered romantic is due to emotional associations and imaginations which surround it. Romanticism is a kind of expressiveness, and what aesthetic value it has is derived value.   The emotional associations that surround the perception of any particular thing often are not explicit.   The object suggests certain emotions, and we do not know why.   We may fill in the indefiniteness with imagination, and the imagery, being itself a measure of indefiniteness, gives rise to further emotions of strange pleasure.   The person who is incurably romantic is one who sees things always surrounded with this haze of emotional imagery.   If this is a source of pleasure to him, as long as the aesthetic attitude is maintained, the object has derived value.

All pleasure aroused in the aesthetic attitude is a measure of the aesthetic value of the object.   If the pleasure is to be found in the perception of the material and form of the object, the value is direct. If the pleasure lies in the expressiveness of the object, that is, in the ways in which the perception of the object is dependent upon knowledge, past experience, or anything else not a part of the object's material and form, the value is derived. Appreciation, however, does not distinguish the sources of its pleasure, nor does it need to. That there is pleasure is sufficient. Further consideration of the sources of pleasure in the aesthetic attitude leads directly into the problem of taste, which will be considered in the next chapter.

One need not know the reasons why he takes pleasure in the perception of an object in order to take that pleasure, but in order to judge that the value appreciated is truly aesthetic, one must be able to identify the aesthetic attitude. An undiscriminating person may not be able to distinguish whether or not he is in this attitude. He may not distinguish whether the pleasure he is experiencing is pleasure in the contemplation of the data of perceptual intuition (no matter if this be "actual" or "imaginative") or pleasure only in the knowledge and associations, memories and emotions that the perception evokes. This lack of discrimination gives rise to aesthetic vulgarity and sentimentality. These subjects will be considered in the next chapter in connection with the problem of taste.

CHAPTER VIII

Taste

1.

Taste is the expression of preference among aesthetic values. Pleasure is the evaluating factor which explains the intensity of aesthetic value; but the scale of intensity is not the same as a standard of preference even though more intense values may usually be preferred. In order to account for preference, it is necessary to take into consideration the reasons why one has the pleasure that leads him to prefer some things to others. Furthermore, once a standard of preference is established, it itself is a factor in determining future pleasures and displeasures. A standard of taste is the measure of preference of aesthetic values. Every individual prefers some kinds of perceptions to others. He may or may not be aware of the principles which govern his preference. If he is aware of them and tries to apply them consistently to the evaluation of his experience, his standard of taste becomes a standard of criticism. Whether it is explicit or not, or whether it is the basis of critical judgments or not, every individual who has preferences which are at all consistent with each other has at least an implicit standard of taste.

A coherent standard of taste is a very complex thing. The preference is there, but upon what is it based, and how has it been formed? Exactly what does this standard imply in the past experience of the individual? How has it been evolved from his previous aesthetic experience? Is it arbitrary? If so, is there any possible understanding of it? If it is not arbitrary, what are the factors which determine it? It is true that preference regarding aesthetic values is exhibited. An adequate understanding of aesthetics cannot be reached until some principles for the explanation of this preference have been found.

Where the term "taste" is used, it is usually with the qualification "good" or "bad." The terms "good taste" and "bad taste" are relative to each other, however, and do not indicate what taste itself is. Taste can be called good or bad only in reference to some standard. Usually the meaning and derivation of the standard is not clear, and if the standard is not clear, the terms "good" and "bad" dependent upon it are not clear.

Often, when persons use the term "good taste," they mean preference based upon a standard which is the embodiment of the cultural and historical judgment of art. Of course, this kind of standard does not throw much light on what taste means. Upon what is the historical judgment of art based?

If it is based upon the recognition of the cultural effect of art upon different civilizations, it is primarily intellectual and cannot be fundamental in aesthetic theory. If it is based upon actual aesthetic and critical judgments passed upon art in past history, the problem is not solved, but remains just the same. What was the standard upon which these judgments were formed?

If the standard is founded upon cultural and historical judgments, there is no basis for introducing innovations in the arts, and there can be no legitimate and genuine change of the standard; for if the innovation be real and not merely specious, or if the standard change, it could be only other than what has been recognized in the past, and if history is the arbiter, it can then be only bad taste. That many persons actually form a standard of taste according to historical judgments of art, despite its palpable inadequacy, is borne out by the fact that they resist innovations in the arts although they profess to be interested in art. Taste does change; genuine judgments of taste and standards of taste change; hence, the standard of taste cannot be based fundamentally upon historical judgments.

"Good taste" is often used to mean merely "in style." This is even more inadequate. What determines the style? Is it determined by aesthetic considerations? If so, what are they? If not, what has it to do with aesthetics, and what warrant has it to be regarded as the basis for a standard of preference among aesthetic values? None of these common uses of the term "good taste" give any solution to the fundamental problem of what the basis of taste really is. The uses of the term "bad taste" do not give any more help, for "bad taste" sometimes means "bad" in reference to a standard, and sometimes means aesthetic vulgarity.

It is a common assumption that taste can be educated or cultivated. Some persons, however, vehemently deny this. Can taste truly be educated? If it can, what are the means to be adopted? These questions indicate an important practical problem which it is impossible to solve unless it be first understood what factors determine preference and upon what aesthetic considerations taste is fundamentally based. It is the business of aesthetics to find out what is really meant by this "taste," which can be either good or bad, and which perhaps can be educated and cultivated.

2.

Taste depends upon sensitiveness to perceptual data. Aesthetic value is based upon the perceptual aspects of phenomena. Therefore, before one can exhibit either good taste or bad taste, he must perceive what there is to be perceived. Before the aesthetic experience is possible at all, one must, at least to some degree, be sensitive to perceptual appearances for their own sakes. A high degree of sensitivity is not ordinary. As has been pointed out, perceptions are usually regarded as signs and symbols of facts.[1] Individuals are constantly compelled to deal with facts, and do not ordinarily pay much attention to perceptions except as signs of facts.

---

[1] See above, Chapter III, Section 4.

As this is the case, it is not usual to perceive all that is to be perceived in any complex situation. Only those parts of the whole perceptual aspect which are sufficient to enable the individual to recognize a situation and to react to it are noted. A chair is a-thing-to-be-sat-on. And usually all we see of a chair is only enough to enable us to recognize it as a-thing-to-be-sat-on. For a person to note more in a situation than is necessary to enable him to cope with it would destroy the economy of his action. Perception, unless it is unusually sensitive, stops at those aspects which enable one to tag a situation, but these, despite their practical and intellectual sufficiency, may be only superficial aspects when the perceptual grasp of the total situation is in question. When one perceives only superficial aspects, his apprehension of the aesthetic values potential in the situation cannot be very adequate.

Any exhibition of taste whatever presupposes an apprehension of aesthetic values. An individual cannot prefer some values to others unless he really experiences them, and a varied preference can be exhibited only in the presence of varied values. Taste, then, is based upon a sensitive apprehension of aesthetic values. In a complex situation, an individual usually perceives what he is in the habit of perceiving; he perceives what he is looking for and what he is acquainted with. This is not full and adequate perception; hence, it is probably that he misses much of the aesthetic value potential in the situation. This lack of sensitiveness is the condition of an undeveloped taste. There is little sensitiveness to aesthetic values unless the powers of perception are highly developed.

3.

Four conditions of sensitiveness and standards of taste dependent upon them. The standard of taste, any standard of taste (as long as it be genuinely aesthetic), is built up from this sensitiveness to aesthetic value. In the development of a complex standard of taste, there are four considerations arising from the degree of sensitiveness of perception. First, the degree of native sensitiveness present has a great influence on preferences. A color-blind person or a tone-deaf person cannot discriminate as much as a person of normal sight or hearing, and he cannot prefer what he cannot experience. Except in these cases of palpable inadequacy of sense organs, native sensitiveness or insensitiveness can be only assumed, for in actual, concrete, complex situations it is impossible completely to separate the native from the acquired. The difference is clearly indicated, however, not only by the fact that in development there must be something to develop, but also by the empirically evident fact that, without any great degree of training or cultivation, the sensitiveness of some individuals is much greater than that of others. Individuals occasionally appear who are unusually gifted. The first condition of taste is this native sensitiveness: the powers of perception must be present and employed. The perceptions must be attended to for their own sakes. This is the prerequisite of all manifestations of preference and standards of taste.

Upon this native sensitiveness a complex development takes

place. Other conditions are added to the first, and actual standards are built up. Much of the pleasure and displeasure which persons find in perception is due to their habits of perception. One accustomed to hear only Occidental music expects, in any complex pattern, certain kinds of chords to follow others. In painting and architecture he expects certain lines to carry out others; and he is displeased if there are no such resolutions or lines. The second consideration, then, in the development of a complex standard of taste is that the individual perceives according to habit. Anything new and strange is apt to escape the sensibility which does not advance beyond the stage where perception is governed merely by habit.

This consideration furnishes a standard of taste: that to which the individual is accustomed is preferred; it is apt to give him more pleasure only because he is accustomed to it. He perceives only what he is used to: the attempt to grasp anything else calls forth an unwonted effort, and is unpleasant. He prefers that which falls into his conventional and habitual perception patterns because he does not adequately perceive anything else. This standard of taste is the most crude and primitive of all standards, and is exhibited usually only by those persons not gifted with much native sensitiveness, or by those whose sensitiveness has been effectively crushed by devotion to the business of living. This standard, of course, differs between different individuals in its specific manifestations, for it is relative to the habits of each individual. It is evidenced in a multitude of ways, but in any way in which it appears, it is incomplete and inadequate, because it is based on only the most superficial exercise of the powers of perception.

Nevertheless, it is probable that most persons do not get far beyond this standard.

The third consideration which makes possible a more complex standard of taste is that the powers of perception become more acute with constant practice. A practiced perception enables one to see more in a situation than he would have seen otherwise. The training of observation is of fundamental importance in the development of any more adequate standard than the first, crude, habitual standard. If one is really interested in seeing all there is to see and becomes practiced in the grasp of complex situations, he begins to see aspects which were not apparent at first. While the apprehension of the most superficial aspects calls forth all the energy that the person whose perception is habitual is wont to exert, one who is interested in the perceptual aspects of objects for their own sake gets used to and perceives easily the more superficial aspects and begins to see others which escaped him before. With the superficial aspects easily grasped, the more profound ones come into view.

The standard of taste based upon practiced and discriminating perception is more advanced than the first or habitual standard. It can be called more advanced because it is built upon the habitual consideration, yet surpasses and replaces it. Habitual perception is still present; no adult can eradicate it, for he perceives in the light of his past experience; but something new and different is added to it. This standard of taste makes possible the apprehension of more intense values than does the first standard. There is more content of perception; there is more activity involved; hence there may be more pleasure.

A practiced perception will apprehend much; but some of the more complex of aesthetic forms will escape even an acute perception unless one has a large background of knowledge and accomplishment to aid his grasp. It was shown by illustration in the previous chapter how knowledge of technique and performance aids the trained musician in perceiving form of which the untrained is unaware.[2] In this case, nonaesthetic aspects of an object influence its perception. Such influences give rise to derived aesthetic values. The full appreciation of many of the more complex, formal elaborations of the arts is not likely without the apprehension of these derived aesthetic values. This brings out the fourth consideration making possible the development of a more complex standard of taste: the apprehension of value may be greatly enhanced and increased through the accretion of the derived aesthetic values which arise from a thorough acquaintance and knowledge of such a situation as that being contemplated.

The fourth condition creates a yet more complete and adequate standard of taste. The person who has a large background and wide acquaintance with which to approach the aesthetic object can appreciate the values potential in that object to a much fuller degree than can the person with small background, for many of the values are derived. This is true, however, only in case the background makes perception more acute and discriminating; that is, only in case the fourth consideration is added to the third. Then and then only can derived aesthetic values be experienced. If the fourth should

2 See above, p. 116.

stand alone and not be in addition to the third, then it is no longer an aesthetic consideration. Thus it may be correctly said that each of these standards of taste is more developed than the ones preceding it, for each is built on the conditions below it and surpasses them only by adding something new by means of which it transcends their limitations.

All these conditions working together in the past environment and experience of the individual determine his standard of preference. Many persons do not advance beyond the crude standard developed from an ungifted native state and habitual perception. Some attain a standard based upon practiced and acute perception. A few attain a standard based not only on sensitive perception but also upon knowledge and background which give rise to the appreciation of derived aesthetic values.

4.

The higher levels of taste further elucidated and illustrated. A more sensitive perception is more discriminating, and a more advanced standard of taste is based on this greater discrimination. For this reason the conditions of the more advanced standards may destroy or lessen the positive intensity of the values that adhere to the superficial aspects of an object. Increased discrimination may disclose other aspects which destroy or mitigate the pleasure that might have been taken in the simpler ones. Hence it cannot be said that a person with a more cultivated taste enjoys all the things that a person with a less cultivated taste does, and other things besides. He enjoys different things, but his enjoyment is based on a more adequate apprehension of what is there.

That which affords pleasure to merely habitual perception may be displeasing to a more adequate and complete perceptual grasp. A chromolithograph may give pleasure to one whose standard of taste is habitual, but perhaps an acute perception can see in it no more than can the habitual perception. To one with the more advanced standard based upon acute perception, the pleasure that might be felt in the apprehension of the superficial aspects is canceled by the dissatisfaction which is felt at the lack of anything but superficial aspects.

This cannot be made a general rule, however. In any particular case it may or may not be true. The taste which finds it impossible *ever* to appreciate more simple or barbaric forms of beauty should be looked at askance. For example, the taste of the musician who finds it impossible under any conditions to discover any degree of aesthetic value in jazz can be put in question. It is doubtful that it is an expression of genuine taste; it may be only an affectation (even though sincere). If it is not an affectation, it is possible that the musician is obtuse to any aesthetic values whatever, even the most superficial. This is true because the more advanced levels of taste are based on the earlier as well as the later conditions; the earlier may be supplanted, but they are never eliminated.

Some objects of the aesthetic attention are very complex. They may not afford much pleasure in the contemplation of their superficial aspects. Their values are appreciated only by a person with acute perception. It has been brought out that a large background may increase the acuteness of perception, and acute perception of the present situation increases the effective background for the realization of future cases. Thus, the third and the fourth conditions of the development of taste interact. If an object is very complex, the more often it is contemplated, the more can be seen in it for this reason. Consider a work such as the play *Hamlet*. There is so much in it that it is impossible to see it at once. And it is impossible ever to see it unless the powers of perception are acute and discriminating and unless one has a large background of knowledge and acquaintance.

The same is true of such a work as the *Divine Comedy*. Because the *Inferno* is spectacular, an undeveloped taste is apt to consider it the best part of the poem. A more advanced taste will see much more value in the *Inferno* than does the undeveloped taste, for there is more to be perceived than the superficial and spectacular aspects; but this more advanced taste will probably consider the *Purgatorio* more poetic than the *Inferno*. The *Purgatorio* is not apt to appeal to the undeveloped taste, because it is not spectacular and there is little pleasure to be derived from its superficial aspects. And yet to the more advanced taste these less superficial values are more intense than are those of the *Inferno*.

One's appreciation of Greek statuary is increased if he knows something about the history and conditions of Greek civilization to help him see what is actually before him. The knowledge may increase the perceptual grasp of the object. In addition to this, it is evident that the statuary could not have any large measure of expressiveness without knowledge of the Greek attitude toward their gods, toward the human body, toward athletic games, and toward sex. If this is true concerning the sculpture of the Greeks, how much more is it true concerning their tragic drama! The conventions of the Greek stage and the conditions of the presentation of the play must be known. Besides these matters of technique, one must know something of the whole depth of Greek thought and the breadth of Greek life that is represented. Preference concerning this drama expressed by one who knows nothing of Greek civilization does not merit attention as a critical judgment.

The higher levels of taste to be attained by the reciprocal interaction of the third and the fourth conditions are reached by but few persons, for the large background required is exceptional. Even those few who do attain this standard in regard to some kinds of art rarely attain it for all kinds. One who is proficient in the technique, practice, and history of one art may be astonishingly ignorant of other arts that are not related to it in technique or history; and even proficiency does not yield an advanced standard of taste unless it is added to acuteness of perception. It is possible for one thoroughly to know the technique and history of an art, and at the same time to be singularly obtuse to the aesthetic values potential in it. He may substitute his knowledge for the apprehension of value. In this case he is not exhibiting any taste which can be called aesthetic at all. The appreciation of technique may give rise to a derived aesthetic value, but not to a direct one, and derived values cannot stand alone.

The standard of taste arising from the exercise of the fourth consideration is more advanced only if knowledge and acquaintance reinforce and complete perceptual apprehension; not if they are substituted for it. Nonaesthetic aspects of an object give rise to derived aesthetic values only if they are secondary to the aspects apprehended in the aesthetic attitude. Thus, derived values always adhere to direct values. Taste that substitutes the appreciation of expressive beauty for formal and material beauty, instead of seeing it merely as enriching and completing the latter, cannot be said to be a highly developed taste, even though it is based on the fourth consideration. In it, the fourth consideration tends too greatly to stand alone and not to be merely the completion of the other conditions. Many ultraromanticists would appear to fill this description. The standard of taste based upon the fourth consideration is more developed than other standards only if it includes all the sensitiveness of perception that may be attained in the development of the other standards.

5.

All genuine judgments of taste are individual. It has often been assumed that there is a sort of universality in the judgment of taste,[3] but each individual's preference is strictly his own, for his perception is based upon his native endowment, past environment, and experience. These factors could hardly be the same for any two individuals; hence the standard of taste is necessarily an individual affair. The apparent universality

---

[3] The classic example of such an assumption is Kant. It must be remembered, however, that he uses the term "judgment of taste," not as a judgment of preference, but as a fundamental judgment of aesthetic value.

arises from the fact that those standards which are based on more adequate perception are truly more complete and advanced than those based on less. This completeness gives a specious appearance of universality. Added to this is the fact that every individual is apt to think that his standard is adequate, because, being unaware of what he does not perceive in a given situation, he naively assumes that what he perceives is all there is. It is evident that any such "subjective universality" is only an error.

All judgments of taste, if they are real judgments and not merely nonsignificant echoes, are statements of individual preference. Of course, anyone's genuine preference may be influenced by the expressed opinion of others if these opinions make him see things that he did not see before. This is the task of the art critic: to point out aspects which others might not see; hence adequate criticism might be expected to alter the individual's genuine judgment. The problems of criticism will be considered later; [4] but at present it is in place to point out that herein lies the possibility of an education of taste. Genuine judgments of taste are individual, but as the standard of taste is based on the sensitiveness of the powers of perception, any consideration (including the expressed opinion of others) which makes a person perceive more in a situation than he perceived before will alter his genuine judgment concerning it. Each added accomplishment develops the acuteness of his perception and his background, and therefore furnishes the conditions for a more advanced standard of taste.

---

[4] See Chapter XI, Sections 1 and 2.

The old saying, "de gustibus non disputandum," has this modicum of truth: judgments of taste are individualistic. The saying may be interpreted in many ways, but it certainly does not mean literally that there is no disputing about matters of taste. Bitter disputes constantly arise. Perhaps the saying would be more true if it said "there is no agreeing about tastes." There is no exact way of settling disagreements about taste, for taste is individual. A judgment of taste is a judgment of individual preference, and if one prefers (or likes) anything, he likes it and there is no disputing that. There is no way to coerce taste by argument. If this is what "de gustibus" means, it is true. It has often been interpreted, however, to mean that there can be no rational analysis or understanding of taste. If it means this, it is false.

Furthermore, if "de gustibus non disputandum" is supposed to mean that taste is necessarily arbitrary, it is false. The standard of taste of any individual is determined by his native sensitiveness, and by the degree that his environment and education and background have increased his sensitiveness to aesthetic value. If habitual perception has been enriched by acute observation and the knowledge which gives rise to the appreciation of derived aesthetic values, the taste is truly more advanced. The steps by which the primitive sensitiveness can be enlarged and enriched can be plainly traced; hence, the determination of a genuine standard of taste is not arbitrary. Any standard which is arbitrary is only a pseudo standard, an affectation.

6.

Highly developed tastes may differ greatly if they are in different historical cultures. It has been pointed out that two different individuals will have different standards. Both of these standards, however, may be on the lowest level or both may be on a higher. Just as it is possible for individual standards to differ, even though they are on the same level, so it is possible for the customary standards of whole cultures and civilizations to differ greatly, even though they are highly advanced. Any advanced standard of taste is built upon the sensitiveness of perception, and it has been pointed out that this sensitiveness is more or less dependent upon the habits of the individual. Perception does not easily grasp a complex situation, all the elements of which are new. There can be wide differences between the customary standards of different civilizations because of the different habits of perception and different backgrounds of these civilizations. An Oriental is not accustomed to look at the world in the same way as is an Occidental. The fundamental tradition of ancient Greek civilization was greatly different in essential respects from that of the civilization of modern Europe. The backgrounds and environments are so different that it is hardly to be expected that the habitual ways of perceiving will be the same. Consequently, it is probable that the standards of two persons in differing cultures will differ more markedly than will those of two in the same culture, even though all the standards considered be on a high level.

Oriental art, for this reason, has remained largely unappreciated by most Occidental peoples. Occidentals of less highly developed standards of taste can never appreciate it, because the Occidental whose perception is only habitual can never see what there is to see in it. The habits of perception of the Oriental are very different from his. A more developed taste can adapt itself more readily, but it is not a foregone conclusion that it will. Chinese music sounds excruciating to most Occidental ears, even to the ears of a person of highly developed taste, until he gets used to it. Then he may apprehend value in it.

When Professor Langfeld says it is questionable that the Greeks took an aesthetic attitude toward their sculpture because it was colored,[5] he is tending to judge a former civilization by present standards. Even this standard is rather limited, as there are evidences in contemporary times that colored statuary may not be so objectionable after all. The point is that the whole cultural tradition of the Greeks was greatly different from that of the present. This caused them to look for and to see in sculpture things quite different from what one now looks for and sees. Who is wrong? Were they wrong, or are we wrong, or is neither wrong? The only sense in which either could be said to be wrong is in the sense of being less complete. Perhaps they did not see all there was to see, and perhaps highly developed tastes now do. These propositions are highly speculative, and in the nature of the case are almost bound to

---

[5] H. S. Langfeld, *The Aesthetic Attitude*, New York, 1920, p. 88.

be mere guesses. Whether or not the Greeks' appreciation was as complete as that of the present, there are sufficient evidences that they took an aesthetic attitude toward their sculpture, and, if one grants the difference in background in their civilization, it cannot be said that the color necessarily inhibited their appreciation. Color might hinder the appreciation of a modern European, but even here there are possibilities of different standards, all on the same level.

7.

The meaning of good taste and bad taste. If the appellation "good taste" means anything in aesthetics, it must indicate something possessed, as his own private possession, by an individual. If any person has good taste, that can mean only that he is sensitive to aesthetic values, and that his standard, whether it be explicit and recognized, or only implicit, is based on this sensitiveness. No individual can significantly be said to have good taste merely because he has consciously adopted a standard generally accepted. Of course, if he has his own genuine standard, it is apt to be similar to some other standard which may or may not be accepted as "cultivated." If it is his only because it is so accepted, it is not genuinely his at all, but is merely affected. All genuine judgments of taste are individual. A cultural standard of taste and a standard "according to style" are only partially or not at all genuine. "Good taste" is not a real exhibition of taste unless it reflects a high degree of sensitiveness in the reaction of the individual.

"Bad taste" means taste which is not acceptable according to a more developed standard. This judgment means nothing either, unless it has reference to sensitiveness (in this case, a relative lack of sensitiveness). And because bad taste is bad only relative to a standard, it is a genuine exhibition of taste, but crude and undeveloped. The primitive sensitiveness does not grasp anything subtle. Take, for instance, the Siwash Indian's taste for color. He loves to paint his house combinations of bright blue and red and green and yellow. This is bad taste according to the standard of most persons, but it does not show a lack of sensitiveness to perceptual appearances. He takes a real delight just in the appearances—a much more genuine delight than does someone who has "adopted" a standard; who paints his house white only because his neighbor's house is white. The Indian's sensitiveness is rather undeveloped and primitive. It has to be struck by something spectacular before it responds.

The term "bad taste" does, then, denote a relative insensitiveness, dullness, or obtuseness to aesthetic values. Good taste and bad taste are relative to each other, and as good taste ought to mean a high degree of sensitiveness, bad taste would mean a degree not so high. Obtuseness to all aesthetic value is probably rather rare, but most persons are obtuse to some kinds of value. Many appreciate painting very highly, but receive no aesthetic pleasure from music. Some appreciate music, but do not apprehend any value in sculpture. Some show a high degree of sensitiveness to aesthetic values in nature, but seem unmoved by most forms of art. An obtuseness to certain kinds of aesthetic value is compatible with an advanced taste in regard to other kinds, because all the factors of native sensitiveness, habits, practice, and background can be different in regard to different kinds of objects.

8.

Aesthetic vulgarity is the confusion of nonaesthetic with aesthetic values. Bad taste is often taken to mean aesthetic vulgarity. This is, in a sense, correct (though it is vague), for if one is highly sensitive to aesthetic values, he is not apt to confuse these values with other considerations; while if he is not very sensitive, he easily falls into confusion. Aesthetic vulgarity is not mere obtuseness; it is a positive confusion of aesthetic values with other values. For example, economic value (often measured by price) does not enhance aesthetic value. A picture or a gem may have a high price owing to its aesthetic value, but its aesthetic value is not due to its price.

Aesthetic vulgarity has no connection with derived aesthetic values. When an intellectual or moral or practical or economic aspect of an object is secondary to the aesthetic aspect, it may give rise to derived aesthetic values. Another value, however, cannot give rise to aesthetic value. Only one kind of value can be apprehended in a situation at one time, for the value is dependent upon the attitude, and only one attitude can be assumed at a time. Derived aesthetic values have nothing to do with aesthetic vulgarity, for aesthetic vulgarity is positive confusion between aesthetic and other kinds of value. It is a reading of aesthetic value in terms of foreign values.

Vulgarity is an error of the evaluative judgment. An object is judged to have aesthetic value, when, in fact, the value is of some other kind. Vulgarity is not an error of the immediate apprehension of value. There can be no error in the apprehension of aesthetic value, but of course, there can be error in any judgment concerning it or the object possessing it. Any judgment can be in error. In case aesthetic vulgarity is being exhibited, some kind of value is being apprehended. Either the aesthetic value is thought to be enhanced by a nonaesthetic value, or else a nonaesthetic value is being apprehended and is thought to be an aesthetic value.

A person who thinks that the beauty of an object is affected by the price of that object is an illustration of the case in which aesthetic value is thought to be enhanced by a nonaesthetic value. Gems can be very beautiful. They often cost a great deal, too. If they are thought to be ornamental because of their cost, vulgarity is being displayed. Despite the cost of diamonds or emeralds, it would be vulgar to wear them with a costume or in surroundings with which they were not in harmony.[6]

A man may be a collector of something, say beautiful pictures or beautiful pottery, or rare books, or perhaps antiques, or even postage stamps. Any one of these occupations may be laudable; but a book does not have aesthetic value because it is a first edition. It may be rare and therefore one may desire to

---

[6] I remember reading a newspaper account a few years ago of a jewel robbery in which the thieves waited in the family garage until a man and his wife returned home late at night. They then removed over $13,000 worth of jewels from the person of the woman. And the couple had been only to a neighborhood moving-picture show!

obtain it, but this has little to do with aesthetics. The collector's interest is not primarily aesthetic, and to think that it is, and that the value of any object for the collector *ipso facto* enhances its aesthetic value, is only to show aesthetic vulgarity.

One may, for any reason at all, have taken a great liking to some kind of modern art. Say, for example, that he is interested in Matisse. Then, if he calls a picture beautiful just because Matisse painted it, he is showing aesthetic vulgarity as truly as if he thinks a book has aesthetic value because it is rare. It may be that the fact Matisse painted it should cause one to look carefully, if he has not appreciated it, for some value which has escaped him. This, however, is another question. To think that one might apprehend value if he discerned carefully enough is not to think that the fact Matisse painted it *ipso facto* gives it aesthetic value. No, a thing does not have aesthetic value merely because it is old, or because it is new, or because a recognized master executed it. These have nothing to do with the question unless they can, through some kind of association, give rise to derived aesthetic value.

An example of the case in which a nonaesthetic value is thought to be an aesthetic value may be found in the evaluation some persons make of art because of its cultural and historical importance. Art is a fundamental part of the culture of any time, and in the study of any historical period or civilization, the art which that civilization produced must be closely scrutinized. All relics from Greek antiquity are highly prized for what they can teach about that civilization. It may be admirable to know these works of art, for the broadening influence that they have enables one to understand periods other than his own. The knowledge of them increases one's own culture. This is culture, however, not aesthetics.[7] To think that the cultural and historical value of a thing is an aesthetic value is to exhibit aesthetic vulgarity. The study of the history of art is an important intellectual discipline, and a knowledge of it is apt to develop one's taste by giving rise to the appreciation of derived aesthetic values, but the study of the history of art is not primarily aesthetic.

Aesthetic vulgarity may be crude or subtle. The confusion of aesthetic value with price is crude. The confusion with sentimental values is crude in the case of the person who thinks ornamental the badly painted portrait of his ancestor in the uniform of an officer in the army of the American Revolution. It is more subtle in the case of the person who likes marine landscapes because he fell in love at the seashore. Confusion of aesthetic values with moral values may be either crude or subtle. It is very subtle in the case of a critic like Ruskin, who always judged beauties by the way that he liked to think of them, rather than by the way they appeared.[8] The cultural or historical confusion is probably the most subtle of all; but the standard of taste that is based upon historical judgments of art is a false standard and is only disguised aesthetic vulgarity.

---

[7] I suspect that the historical aspects of art greatly influenced Hegel's aesthetic theory. See Hegel, *Philosophy of Fine Art,* Introduction, translation by B. Bosanquet, London, 1905, top of p. 49.

[8] See Ruskin, *Modern Painters,* Everyman's Edition, Vol. III, p. 110.

CHAPTER IX

Art

1.

The definition of art. Aesthetic value inheres in the perceptual aspects of phenomena. Both natural and constructed objects have perceptual aspects. Hence, aesthetic value may be found both in nature and in objects constructed by man. In common speech, objects due to human construction are contrasted with those which are not by being called artificial. Among the various kinds of artificial products are those that seem to have been constructed especially for the purpose of being sources of aesthetic value. These are usually called "art," or "fine art." They may or may not have values other than aesthetic, but at least they have aesthetic value. The study of aesthetics is concerned with the constructive activity of man in so far as this activity produces objects having aesthetic value.

Art, then, or aesthetic art, is a vehicle which conveys aesthetic values. The term "vehicle" is used to point out that art is a construction which carries or transports some commodity from place to place. In this case, the commodity transported is positive aesthetic values, and the places are individual sensibilities. An artist conveys to another a sense of aesthetic value (or a vision of value) which is intimately his own. He does this by means of a composition, the contemplation of which awakens the sense of value in the beholder.

It would not be accurate, however, to say that art is a vehicle which is constructed for the *purpose* of conveying aesthetic values. It matters less what the purpose is than whether it actually conveys values. It must *successfully* accomplish its intended function of awakening the aesthetic experience in the beholder. The vehicle and the vision of value are both important. If the vision has no vehicle, it is not art, no matter how intense it is. If the vehicle contains no vision, it is not art, no matter how well it is constructed. A man may have the desire and purpose to write the best poem in the world, and may write something in the form of a poem, but it is not art unless it conveys aesthetic values. If the work *does* convey aesthetic values, it *is* art, again no matter what the purpose. Johnson may have written *Rasselas* to pay for his mother's funeral, but it may be art despite this ulterior purpose. It is art if it conveys those aesthetic values realizable in that form of literature.

The purpose of the artist may be "to express himself," but even the fact that he thinks he has expressed himself does not make the product of his activity art. It is important to consider whether what he had to express was aesthetic, and whether it was worth expressing. If his purpose was to "express his feelings," again, whether the resultant product is art depends on what those feelings were and how well they are expressed. If his purpose was to "create beauty," it all depends on what he thinks beauty is, and whether his production succeeds in awakening an aesthetic experience in his audience.

The artist must have a vision of value. This is often called his "inspiration," though this word must be used with circumspection. The artist sees something in the appearance of the landscape that his neighbor does not see, or he hears harmonies that his neighbor does not hear. It matters no whit whether he actually perceives them or only imagines them. As has been pointed out above, the distinction between actual perception and perceptual imagination is irrelevant to the aesthetic experience.[1] One man looks into the sky and has a vision of the moon. His more imaginative neighbor passes the graveyard and has a vision of ghosts. The first man calls his vision real and that of his neighbor imaginary. Both are perceptual. The artist creates an external embodiment for his vision, and if, upon contemplation, this embodiment succeeds in reawakening the vision or in awakening a similar vision, it is art. The construction of the vehicle is a matter of technique. If the technique is not mastered well enough for the vehicle to convey what it is supposed to convey, then it is not art. The success of the vehicle in conveying values is of primary importance, and the only criterion of this success is the amount of pleasure to be gained in the perceptual apprehension of the object. Pleasure in perceptual apprehension is the measure of

---

[1] See above, Chapter III, Section 6.

asthetic value; hence the more pleasure in the perceptual apprehension, the more successful the art.

2.

Criticism of the view that art is an activity. Art has often been defined in the history of aesthetics, not as a thing, an object, but as an activity of the human spirit.[2] In the present study this usage will not be followed; the term will be used as the generic name of a class of objects. Art, in the present study, means a work of art. Poems, pictures, musical compositions, pieces of sculpture, and architecture are characteristically called art. There are striking differences between objects constructed by human artifice and natural objects. It is convenient and useful that these differences be noted by aesthetic analysis and reflected in its terminology.

To define art as an activity of the human spirit does not accurately express the relation of art to the aesthetic experience. The aesthetic experience is an experience of value. There is an objective term entering into the relation from which the value emerges. This objective term is the perceptual aspect of some real or imagined object. If the object is not due to human construction, it is called natural; if it is, it is called art. It is the object, the thing, the work of art which is important in this relation, not the activity or process of constructing it.

---

[2] See Ducasse, *Philosophy of Art,* New York, 1929, p. 15. See also, Croce, *Aesthetic,* London, 1922, p. 51; and "Breviary of Aesthetic," published in Rice Institute, *Book of the Opening,* Vol. II, p. 436.

To define art as an activity is to confuse the field of aesthetics with that of ethics. "Moral" means concerned with modes of activity, and the philosophic study of the field of morals is ethics. The understanding of activity in pursuit of ends is a function of moral philosophy; hence, to define art as a unique activity in pursuit of unique ends would be to place the philosophy of art in ethics. This is the case no matter whether the activity is defined as expression in pursuit of the end of self-objectification, or as some other activity in pursuit of some other end. A study of art following from such a definition would not be aesthetics no matter how valuable it might be in some other branch of philosophy.

To define art as an activity and then to suppose that such a definition is in harmony with a system of aesthetics is to suppose (implicitly or explicitly) either that aesthetics is a division of ethics, or that the artist's experience in the creation of art is the characteristic example of the aesthetic experience. The latter alternative, if analyzed thoroughly, would itself be reduced to the former; but because it is rarely explicit and is not analyzed where it is assumed, it must be considered as a separate question.

3.

Analysis of the artist's activity. It seems obvious that the artist must feel an intensity of the aesthetic experience not vouchsafed to the common man. If it were not so, how could he portray the beauties which are to be found in his art?

In consequence of this, it has appeared to many that the experience of the artist should be taken as the characteristic example of the aesthetic experience. The artistic experience, however, is very complex—so complex, in fact, that few artists have been able to analyze their own working with any great degree of success. It contains many factors that are not primarily aesthetic. Hence, to take it as the most characteristic aesthetic experience is to invite confusion.

In the first place, the experience of the artist is primarily an activity: he is engaged in producing something. It does not matter whether his production is to be classed as "work" or "play"; it is production nevertheless. Nor does it matter whether the production is an endeavor to copy something or not; still it is production. The work of art may be that "which in a unique way corresponds to something that was not an object at all, viz., to a feeling." [3] Yet to produce it requires the exercise of an activity aimed at copying something, even though that something is not a material entity. If this activity is successfully pursued, it implies the ability to use means to accomplish a desired end.

The artist has an aesthetic vision (or a feeling, in the terms of the quotation above), but he is concerned with many things other than this vision. His ability to use means to produce the desired end of "objectifying" or "expressing" this vision (or feeling) is technique. Technique, as the knowledge of means to produce an end, is intellectual. Hence, if the artist's activity were a characteristic example of the aesthetic experi-

---

[3] C. J. Ducasse, *Philosophy of Art,* New York, 1929, p. 108. Cf. the whole of his Chapter VII for an illuminating discussion of various play theories of art.

ence, a large part of the aesthetic experience would be intellectual. In addition, aside from the knowledge involved in technique, the actual practice of technique, as the attainment of ends, is practical and moral. Hence, if the artist's activity were the best example of the aesthetic experience, another large part of that experience would be practical and moral.

This kind of view displays hopeless confusion. The only part of the artist's experience which is truly aesthetic in his vision of value. If he creates an embodiment or vehicle for that vision, that is another matter, and does not add anything to the aesthetic nature of the vision.[4] The vision (or "inspiration") may not burst full blown on the artist, but may come gradually as the result of experimentation with technique, but this again is irrelevant. It does not matter how the artist gets his inspiration. He may get it by shutting himself up in a cold room and letting his imagination loose, or by observing the active drama of the world, or by taking alcohol or opium. This would be relevant to morals, but not to aesthetics, because the aesthetic attitude is not concerned with any of these ulterior matters. The activity of the artist may be practical or moral or immoral in the most narrow sense, and still he may produce works of art. Religious painters and didactic poets have often produced real art. Bunyan probably had an ardent desire to save souls when he wrote the *Pilgrim's Progress*. Tolstoy, al-

---

[4] This is the truth which Croce states obscurely and confusedly when he says that the artist's construction of a technical medium adds nothing to his expression. See B. Croce, *Aesthetic,* translation by Ainslie, London, 1922, pp. 50, 96–97. The present study does not define the aesthetic experience in terms of expression as does Croce. The relation between the present theory and Croce is discussed in Appendix C.

though he misunderstood the principles and purposes of his own art, nevertheless produced art.

It is impossible to take the artist's experience as the characteristic example of the aesthetic experience, not only because of these theoretic difficulties, but also because of the practical consideration that the experience of the artist in the purely aesthetic field is apt to be very narrow. He is concerned with only one or a few kinds of art, and his vision is apt to be confined to these kinds. He may be full of artistic prejudices. He may not be concerned with aesthetic value as a whole. Aesthetic value can be found in nature as well as in art, but the artist may not be interested in nature. It is inevitable that confusion be introduced into any theory of aesthetics which goes to the creative experience of the artist for the solution of its problems.

It is evident now that the definition of aesthetics as the philosophy of art is not adequate. If the philosophy of art is the philosophy of skilled activity, only a part of that activity is relevant to aesthetics; aesthetics and such a philosophy of art would overlap. If the philosophy of art is the philosophy only of aesthetic art, then it is only a part of aesthetics. It would coincide with aesthetics only in case art were defined as the artistic object and aesthetic values could be found nowhere else than in this object. A complete philosophy of art would include the principles of the creation and production, of the appreciation, and of the criticism of art. Even here there would not be a complete theory of aesthetics. The primary consideration is: *what is meant by aesthetic and by aesthetic value?* This question cannot be answered by an investigation only of art and the appreciation of art. Aesthetic art can be distinguished from other kinds only on the basis of a previous understanding of this question.

4.

Criticism of the view that art is expression. Art is not adequately defined by saying that it is expression. In the first place, the term "expression" is itself ambiguous, and may refer to either an activity or an object. As art is best defined as an object (or, rather, as the generic name for a class of objects), it is not necessary to consider the meaning of the term "expression" as intending an activity. To express means to render sensible; hence an expression is anything wherein a mental content is revealed or is put into an objective form so that it may be communicated. It is not necessary that external communication take place. It is necessary only that the mental content be given form which renders it communicable. Obviously, the only test for successful expression is to see whether its form accomplishes that for which it is intended. The only criterion of expression is communication.[5]

Art is expression, but this alone does not make it art. It is expression, for it renders a mental content into sensible form whereby it can be communicated. The mental content in this case is the vision of value, and the form is the technical construction. Art is expression, but expression of what? There is no

---

[5] Croce is the greatest exponent among contemporary writers of the view that art is expression. He has had great influence. A discussion of his views and those of Carritt, one of his English followers, and their relation to the present study will be found in Appendix C.

definition unless this question is answered. Expression of abtract meanings is not art. If it were, a treatise on higher mathematics would be art. It may be true, but it is not definitive to say that art is the expression of emotion. A moral, or practical, or sentimental emotion is not transfused into something aesthetic by the fact that it has taken on the form wherein it may be communicated. If a moral emotion is communicated from one person to another, it remains moral all the time. If the second person receives something aesthetic, he receives something other than that which the first individual intended to communicate, and no adequate communication has taken place. If art is the expression of emotion, it must be stipulated that it is the expression of aesthetic emotion. It has been remarked above that it is not satisfactory to define aesthetics in terms of emotion or feeling.[6] If art is expression, it is aesthetic expression, and one is thrown back on a previous analysis of the meaning of "aesthetic."

Art is expression, but it is the expression of an aesthetic vision. The artist has the experience of aesthetic value, and he embodies this vision in forms which make it communicable to others (or to himself). To tell others that he has an aesthetic vision is not to create art, for it does not put his experience into communicable form. Whatever communication there is in the telling is intellectual; but to construct something by means of which his experience may be in some measure transferred to another is to create art.

Art is expression, but it is the expression of aesthetic values.

---

[6] See above, Chapter III, Sections 8 and 9.

Even here it would be more accurate to say that the work of art *embodies* aesthetic values. Art is the constructed object which succeeds in awakening a vision of value in the beholder. The important point is that before it can be called art the attempted expression must be able to pass the test of conveying values. Art could be defined then, as successful expression of aesthetic values, when by successful is meant an expression which actually does convey the sense of value from the artist to another (or to himself). It is preferable, however, to emphasize the conveyance of value and to omit altogether the term "expression" in the definition of art. Thus confusion with "expressive beauty," which has been given a clear meaning by Santayana and which is used with that meaning in the present study, can be avoided. It may be that all art has expressive beauty in Santayana's sense of the term, but this is not its defining characteristic.

5.

The nature and critical judgment of art is social as well as individual. As the apprehension of all aesthetic value is individual, and as the appreciation of art is apprehension of aesthetic value, the appreciation of art is individual. It is the individual's own sensibility which gives rise to the values he experiences. He cannot appreciate the art of that in which he can apprehend no aesthetic value; but this is only half the story. The appreciation of actual value is individual, but the potentiality of value does not depend upon particular temporal and individual conditions. There may be an intellectual appraisal of the existence of potential value. In other words, a given object may not convey values to a certain person, but perhaps he can convince himself that it does convey values to others. To that extent, he has to call it art, even though he cannot appreciate it. Art is a vehicle which conveys values not only to one individual but to others. From art is expected a community of appreciation, for its success as art is measured by its adequacy of conveyance. If it can convey values only to one person, then its conveyance is not as adequate as if it could convey values to many persons. Hence, art, by its definition, is social as well as individual. A work is good art to the extent that it conveys values not only to one or a few observers, but to many. It must be borne in mind, however, that the observers who count are those whose appreciation is sensitive and whose standard of taste is developed.

Anyone passing critical judgments upon art must be able to estimate potential values in it, even though he cannot realize or appreciate them. This is intellectual. All critical judgments of art are intellectual. The actual appreciation is aesthetic, but the critical estimate is evaluative. One may, because of some peculiar prejudice or blindness, fail to see any aesthetic value in the work of Euripides or Plato, but in a cold intellectual way he can realize that others see it. If he knows enough about the aesthetic experience and the external signs of this experience to assure himself that others are apprehending aesthetic value, and if he knows enough about the particular kind of art under consideration to be able to recognize the possibilities of value in it, then he must admit that this work which others are appreciating is art, even though he cannot realize the values in it himself. He can call it art without dissimulation, although he must add that he himself does not appreciate it. In judging that a work is or is not art, one is judging whether or not it falls under a particular definition. This is intellectual. The exhibition of appreciation and taste is not intellectual, but the critical estimation is.

6.

The judgment that a work of art is great art is based on history. Art can be called truly great or catholic only when it is an adequate vehicle for the conveyance of aesthetic values not only to many individuals of one period of culture, but to many periods as well. One does not have to be a Greek or a philosopher to apprehend aesthetic value in Euripides or Plato. The appeal of some works of art, however, may be limited to those beholders in some particular culture, and with a definite background. One would hardly call such works of art great or catholic. For example, some of the dramas of Ibsen are rather limited to a particular social system and particular social problems. The appreciation of such art presupposes that the beholder has the knowledge of the situations and problems with which the art deals. A large part of its values may be derived values. Now such an art may be very fine in the sense that to those who do have the requisite knowledge the values are intense, but the large proportion of derived values dependent upon a particular background necessarily makes its appeal limited.

To one who knows poetry and knows it well, much of Keats'
poetry is exquisite; but because its appeal is limited, it should
hardly be called catholic. Perhaps those with a very advanced
taste will always appreciate it. Only with this qualification can
it be called great.

A piece of contemporary art can hardly be called great with
any degree of certainty. The critic may not be able to see
that its appeal is limited to knowledge of local characteristics
of the present civilization, and that it will not convey aesthetic
values to those outside this civilization. The judgment that
any piece of art is great art is an historical judgment and is apt
to be influenced by considerations which are not wholly relevant
to aesthetics.[7] Such a judgment may not be at all useful as a
guide to the individual's appreciation. The fact that multitudes
have found value in a work should indicate to a person that
if he looks closely and carefully enough he will find value too;
but there is no guarantee that he will find it. The aesthetic
value is independent of the number of individuals who have
appreciated it. To think that the aesthetic value of a work
consists in the fact that many have found value in it is only
aesthetic vulgarity.[8]

Because the judgment that any work of art is great art is primarily an historical judgment, there is apt to be a certain
amount of resistance from critics to any radical innovation in
art. This is loudly supported by those persons whose stand-

---

[7] When, after the lapse of a generation or so, we begin to make collections
of art, we do so not so much for the aesthetic value as for the historical, cultural,
and autobiographical information contained therein.

[8] Furthermore, such an assumption is inconsistent with itself. Many persons
make it, nevertheless.

ard of taste has not advanced beyond the habitual level. Many recent productions created a furore upon their appearance. Some called them art. Others called them rubbish. The dispute boiled down to a dispute over art forms rather than over particular works. A man may not be able to appreciate a Matisse because of a hidebound academic training or because of his inability to see form behind representation. He may not be able to appreciate the Impressionists because he is color-blind. He may not be able to appreciate a composition by Debussy because it is complex and scintillating, while he is simple and sentimental. If he knows something about painting or music, however, and if he can assure himself that these unusual looking or sounding compositions really convey aesthetic values to other people, he must recognize that to that extent they are truly art. If he thinks otherwise he is merely mistaken in his judgment. Anything that acts as the vehicle for the conveyance of aesthetic value is art.

7.

The distinction between pure and mixed art does not yield an hierarchy of the arts. Attention has been called to the fact that any phenomenon may have many different aspects.[9] Any given work of art, besides being a conveyance for aesthetic values, may have meaning, or be of use, or be morally edifying. To the extent to which the aesthetic aspects of any kind of art are

---

[9] See above, Chapter VII, Section 3.

accompanied by other aspects, that kind of art is impure or mixed. To the extent to which the aesthetic aspects are less accompanied by other aspects, that kind of art may be called pure. For example, poetry and other sorts of literature are relatively mixed art, because they have intellectual meaning and moral significance in addition to their aesthetic value. Fine pottery may be highly artistic, but the art of pottery is a mixed art, for pottery has use. Music is a relatively pure art, though it is not wholly pure, as there may be representational and sentimental elements in it; and there are intellectual aspects even in the most sensuous music. An intellectual attitude is taken toward it when its technique is considered.

Within any particular kind of art the same principle of classification may be applied. For example, lyric poetry is more nearly pure art than is drama, which in turn might be expected to be more pure than the novel. It might be supposed possible to construct a relative graded scale ranging from music, as one of the most pure forms, through painting and literature to the crafts such as pottery, and to strictly applied art, but such a scale would not be exact, and would be of very little use in aesthetics. Any kind of art is subject to wide variations of treatment. In the first place, poetry might differ greatly in purity according to whether it is lyric, epic, didactic, and so forth. Painting might differ greatly according to whether it is formal, representational, dramatic, or historical. In this case a lyric poem could conceivably be purer than an historical painting. Music differs in purity according to whether it is classic, romantic, sentimental, or descriptive. In order to form an exact scale of purity, it would be necessary to subdivide the arts to take account of all these differences until at last one came down to the particular work of art. All critical judgments are, in the last analysis, based on particular works of art; hence all dicta concerning art forms are only rough generalizations.

This distinction of relatively pure from relatively mixed art does not constitute an hierarchy of the arts. In the first place, it is not exact as a generalization, and in the second place it forms no basis for a scale of evaluation. Pure art cannot be said *a priori* to be better than mixed art. The final evaluation must always be of the particular work of art, and a given novel may be a better conveyance of aesthetic values than a given poem. Just because it is a novel and more mixed does not make a good novel worse than a poor poem. It is this fact which makes any attempt at an aesthetic hierarchy of the arts somewhat absurd. That which is better in art can be measured only by adequacy in conveyance of aesthetic values. There is always the possibility that in the more mixed forms the direct values will be reinforced by derived values. The piece of pure art, in any given case, might be thin and tenuous, even though relatively successful in conveying those values it attempts to convey, while the piece of mixed art might be rich and abundant in derived values.[10]

---

[10] Mixed art must not be confused with what is usually called the "combined arts." The latter term refers to arts like those of the theater and opera, which combine several different media in order to produce their effect. See D. W. Prall, *Aesthetic Judgment*, New York, 1929, Chapter XII.

8.

The spirit and atmosphere of art is dependent upon suggested imagery, often of the "lower senses." The recognized and established forms of art all appeal primarily to sight and hearing. There have been attempts to make such things as a symphony of wines, but the problems of technique seem to be insurmountable. The senses of taste and smell evolutionally are not as developed as are those of sight and hearing. There is less power of discrimination, and therefore a varied richness of formal structure in taste and smell would hardly seem possible. Furthermore, the organs themselves are harder to reach and appeal to with a varied stimulus than are the organs of the more developed senses. The factors of sensational adaptation to stimuli, and of change by contrast, and of "hangover" of stimuli are very different in taste and smell than in sight and hearing. All these difficulties militate against the perceptual grasp of a varied stimulus, and make it improbable that any art of the "lower" senses will appear. It is also true that there seems to be no apparent order natural to the sensations of taste and smell which would offer the structural foundation for a complex elaboration of form, and before any art of taste or smell could appear, some way of ordering the materials would have to be found.[11] In case, however, that an ordering principle became apparent, the remaining difficulties would be

---

[11] Cf. D. W. Prall, *Aesthetic Judgment,* Chapter V.

technical, and if they should be mastered, new arts would be born. It cannot be maintained that the "lower" senses are intrinsically unsuitable for art.

Art is very complex, and often contains an appeal to the "lower" senses. Actual and suggested sensations and images from the "lower" senses are present in its appreciation. Anything which increases pleasure in the aesthetic attitude contributes to aesthetic value, and stimulations of the "lower" senses may supply such pleasure. The clearest case, perhaps, is the appeal to touch through texture in sculpture, painting, and architecture. But the appeal to kinaesthetic empathy is also a clear example of the relevance of the "lower" senses to the appreciation of art. Sensations of smell, sometimes even sensations of taste, but certainly organic sensations such as the feeling of fresh air in the lungs, have a great deal to do with the appreciation of aesthetic value in some kinds of natural landscape, such as mountain scenery. These sensations and images can be suggested in art by a subtle use of technique, and in frankly representational art the aesthetic value is greatly increased by such suggestion. Keats and Byron were masters of such suggestion in the realms of poetry.

It is the richness of suggested images, a large proportion of which are of the "lower" senses, that makes the spirit and atmosphere of representational art. The spirit in art is what seems to make it live and move, but it is often difficult intellectually to appraise it. One can usually "feel" [12] the difference between two works which are similar in many respects except

---

[12] This means "feeling," not in the sense of "emotion," but in the sense of "perceptual apprehension." See above, Chapter III, Section. 9.

that one seems to be full of spirit and the other is dead and lifeless, but one can rarely state the reasons for the difference clearly. The difference often lies in the abundance of suggested images of the "lower" senses. The work which is full of spirit and atmosphere is full of suggested images. Some painters can paint snow so that it looks cold. This is obviously a figure of speech, for cold is not the name of a visual sensation. The point is that the painter paints in such a way that his work suggests incipient imagery of cold sensations. The suggested imagery is often the only discernible reason for the difference between a really first-rate work of art and a second- or third-rate work. These images enter into the perceptual grasp of the first-rate work and make that grasp more complete. They enrich and make full the perception, and increase the pleasure in the aesthetic attitude.

9.

The place of representation in art. What place has representation in art? Is art essentially representative, as Plato and Aristotle seemed to hold? Or is representation utterly irrelevant to fine art, as some contemporary writers seem to hold? These questions recently have been argued at great length, especially in regard to painting. The naive attitude is that that which is not good representation is not good painting. One often hears a person in a gallery of modern art exclaim, "That does not look like any landscape I ever saw"; and therewith the would-be critic disposes of the picture under consideration. He supposes that if it is not good representation it cannot be good art.

This kind of naive criticism has led Clive Bell, among others, to maintain that "the representative element . . . can do the picture no good and it may do it harm." [13] The attempt to find representation in the work of art, and the criticism of the fidelity of representation are characteristics of only the uncultured critic; and the attempt to achieve representation is a characteristic of only the charlatan artist, according to this view.

Although Bell's position is extreme, there is something to be said for it, because the judgment of fidelity of representation is an intellectual judgment. Representation in painting, or in any other art, is bad if it diverts the attention from the aesthetic attitude; and there can be no doubt that if often does so. If one's attention is directed not primarily toward the grasp of the perceptual data which is before him, but toward the comparison of this data to some other, imagined or remembered, he is not in the aesthetic attitude.[14] If one makes a judgment of verisimilitude, or of the fidelity of representation in a work of art, and thinks that this is evaluating the art as art, he is exhibiting aesthetic vulgarity. It may be crude or it may be subtle vulgarity, but it is vulgarity because it is confusing an intellectual experience with an aesthetic one. It might be unfortunate that a nonrepresentative picture, or a picture whose representation is distorted, is hung with landscapes or given

---

13 Clive Bell, *Art*, London, 1914, p. 226.

14 I am, of course, using "perceptual" to refer to perceptual intuition, not perception of fact, as defined in Chapter III, Section 4.

the name of a landscape. This, however, is beside the question of whether or not it is good art.

Representation cannot be bad in art unless it diverts the aesthetic attitude. Whether or not art is representative is of less importance than its adequacy in conveying aesthetic values. To suppose that representation is necessary is to suppose that the only real sources of aesthetic values are natural objects; thus, if art is to convey aesthetic values, it must copy natural objects. On the other hand, to suppose that art must not or cannot be representative is to deny all aesthetic value to natural objects. If natural objects can have aesthetic value, then the representation of them in art can have aesthetic value. As both natural and constructed objects can have aesthetic value, any art may be representative and yet be good art, but no art need be representative.

There are aesthetic values in nature, and selection such as the artist exercises can enhance these values. Selection is wholly compatible with representation. It is compatible with even a high degree of representation, but not with exact verisimilitude. The recognition of this fact is the major modification which Aristotle made in Plato's mimetic theory of art; and it makes it a much more adequate theory.

Representation may *contribute* to the total value of any situation, but to suppose that it *constitutes* the value is to exhibit aesthetic vulgarity. Representative features in a complex composition give a familiarity to the complexity which enables one to grasp it in perception much more adequately.[15] It may be

---

[15] See above, Chapter IV, Section 4.

improbable that one will grasp a very complex design in painting unless the design is based on some representative features, no matter how conventionalized or even distorted these may be.[16]   In arabesque, where there are no representative features, there must be a great deal of repetition in the grouping of the lines to enable perception to grasp the complexity.

It must also be remembered that representation may be a source of derived values.[17]   Almost all of the common expressiveness of such arts as painting and literature and sculpture is dependent upon representation.   Derived aesthetic values may even arise from the appreciation of the skill and craftsmanship of representation, but one must guard against aesthetic vulgarity here.   A high degree of representation is apt to lead the careless observer to perceive facts, and one who naively criticizes painting adversely if it is not good representation is probably looking only or mainly for facts, and thus is not in the aesthetic attitude.   The perception of fact is intellectual.   And a *mere* consideration of skill and craftsmanship is intellectual also.   A slight shift in attitude, if the observer supposes that he is still concerned with aesthetic value, will result in aesthetic vulgarity.   And it is difficult for one whose standard of taste is based on the level of habitual perception to avoid this shift.   Hence, there is danger in too literal a degree of representation in art.

---

[16] A striking illustration of this can be found in the painting by Franz Marc called *Mandrill*.

[17] See above, Chapter VII, Section 5.

10.

The nature of style in art. The term "style" is used in various ways in the description of art and of the artist. It has been used to denote everything from habitual tricks of technique to that which is uniquely and inescapably original in the work of art. The first use is handy in historical generalizations, as when one speaks of the Byzantine style, or the style of the High Renaissance. Such expressions are only roughly indicative of very general tendencies, and are not useful except in rough descriptions. If any period in the history of art has achieved a style, it is because the artists of that period have achieved a unique way of looking at things. The style of a period is apparent only because of certain general tendencies which the artists of that period show in common. Behind these general tendencies are the particular differences that each artist has, and we can speak of a period style only by overlooking these differences which are usually of superlative importance in making 'the work of the artist really first-rate art.

The difference between the work of a great artist and lesser artists usually lies right here: that the great artist has achieved a unique and individual style which makes his work live. It can be parodied but not reproduced by others. This style is based primarily on the way that the artist perceives things. He has achieved an original view which is shown in his art. The aesthetic vision is pre-eminently individual, and each artist sees things in his own way. If he has great vision and apprehends intense values, he will have a style of his own. The source of the style is the aesthetic vision. If he perceives things intensely and individually, and in a characteristic manner, this will be reflected in a characteristic manner of handling technique. This handling of technique is often called style, but that it is not the essence of style is shown when two artists fall into the same habits of technique. The fact that the individual way that the artist perceived things in the essence of his style explains why, although one artist can be influenced by another's style, it is so utterly impossible for him adequately and sufficiently to copy it. Style cannot be attained by technical manipulation alone. It can be obtained only by achieving a characteristic way of perceiving things. Art is a vehicle for the conveyance of aesthetic values. First comes a vision of values, and then comes the technical construction of a vehicle. Unless the vision is intense and characteristic, the construction of the vehicle is of no account. If the vision is characteristic and intense, its originality will be reproduced in the vehicle, and the art will have style.

11.

The place of subject matter in art. A subject matter for art is not eminently more fitting or less fitting according to whether or not it has great scope. A large work of art, or a work having a wide scope of subject matter, cannot be said *a priori* to convey greater aesthetic values than a small or lesser one. Adequacy of conveyance is not dependent upon the size of the vehicle.

It has been pointed out that aesthetic values cannot be ordered according to their scope.[18] Hence a work of art on a large scope is not necessarily of greater aesthetic value than one on a small scope. The only way to tell whether or not it is of more value is to experience it. It is patently absurd to say that the pleasure of experiencing it will necessarily be more intense just because the work is large. Intensity is not extensity. The only way that a large scope can influence the merit of a work of art is through derived aesthetic values. It is much more difficult to preserve the unity which is the essential of perceptual grasp; hence, if the large scope is handled well, one may admire the skill and craftsmanship exhibited. There is more opportunity to convey aspects from which derived aesthetic values may be obtained. However, when derived values become proportionately large, the same caution against aesthetic vulgarity must be made here as always.

If art is anything that conveys aesthetic values, and if aesthetic values may be found in anything perceptual, then nothing with perceptual aspects is, in its own nature, impossible of use as subject matter of art. It is sometimes held that there are certain subjects, whether garbage cans or pornography, which are intrinsically unsuitable as the subject matter of art. It may be that there are some subjects toward which it is very difficult for some persons to take the aesthetic attitude, because other biologically more impelling attitudes intrude. These persons, then, cannot appreciate any aesthetic value in a work of art with such a subject matter, but the fact that it is im-

---

[18] See above, Chapter V, Section 8,

possible for them to assume the aesthetic attitude is no indication that there are and can be no values potential. If it is difficult or impossible to take an aesthetic attitude toward some subject matter, perhaps that subject matter is best avoided. That does not make it intrinsically nonaesthetic. The works of Rabelais may be fine art despite the fact that some parts of them are obscene. Just because someone does not like to think of garbage cans is no indication that such objects may not have aesthetic value. In all strictness, his not liking to think about them might have something to do with *his* apprehension of aesthetic value, but it has little to do with the potentiality of aesthetic value.

If all subject matter toward which it is difficult for persons of undeveloped taste to maintain the aesthetic attitude had been avoided, the history of art would be robbed of some of its choicest works. The problems arising from the use of such subject matter in art will be discussed in the next chapter under the heading "difficult beauty."

CHAPTER X

Difficult Beauty and Ugliness

1.

The problem of difficult beauty stems from Aristotle. The subject matter of tragic art may be strikingly different in kind from that of idyllic or lyric art. This is so apparent that its observation called forth the first separate philosophical writing in aesthetics—Aristotle's *Poetics*. In Chapter IV of the *Poetics,* Aristotle notes that we "delight to contemplate" the representation of forms which in themselves would be sources of displeasure, such as "the forms of the most ignoble animals, and of dead bodies." The fact that it sometimes gives pleasure to contemplate things which at other times (or, as Aristotle thought, in their own nature) are unpleasant, seemed to him to call for explanation.

The heart of the problem could be found in tragic drama. Tragedy portrays situations of predominating pain, but despite this fact, there may be profound pleasure in witnessing tragedy. The *Poetics* is concerned with the theory of tragedy, and assumes that it is necessary to explain how the contemplation of tragic drama can yield pleasure. The whole statement of the problem, as well as its treatment, is bound up with Aristotle's representative theory of art. For him, art is the representation either of actual or of universalized situations. Aesthetic pleasure is the pleasure of recognizing a representation, or perhaps of recognizing the universal elements in what is represented. If the actual situation is unpleasant, why is not its representation unpleasant? This, for Aristotle, was the major problem of the theory of tragedy.

The feeling that there is a difference between the subject matter of lyric art, on the one hand, and of tragic art, the grotesque, the sublime, and so forth, on the other, was intensified by the seventeenth-century dislike for Gothic art. It was brought to conscious realization by the romantic movement in the latter part of the eighteenth and beginning of the nineteenth centuries. The romantics presented "new beauties" that seemed wild and barbarous to the cultured civilization of the time. Even Goethe, an early leader in the new movement, in his old age spoke disparagingly of the newer school of "graveyard poets." In his earlier leadership, Goethe had distinguished between the beautiful and the characteristic as themes which art might use. Kant distinguishes between the beautiful and the sublime. Constantly, there is an attempt to distinguish between that kind of aesthetic subject matter the pleasure in which is "natural," and that kind the pleasure in which must in some way be explained and justified.

The problem recently has been explicitly stated and discussed with critical acumen by Bosanquet in *Three Lectures on Aesthetic*.[1]   DeWitt H. Parker discusses it at length both in his *Principles of Aesthetics* and in his *Analysis of Art* under the heading, "The Problem of Evil in Aesthetics."[2]   It has been implicitly emphasized also by the radical departures from tradition in contemporary art.   Many so-called "modern tendencies" in art make use of subject matter and methods of portrayal which seem to many persons harsh and inharmonious, or even "positively ugly."

2.

Analysis of the Problem.   Before the solution of this problem can be reached, it must be stated accurately and clearly.   Its usual statement (which the foregoing paragraphs have briefly indicated) is far from clear.   Exactly what is the problem here?   In so far as it concerns aesthetics, it is not primarily a problem of art creation.   It goes beyond the questions involved in art creation, for the romantic school discovered the beauties of nature in her wilder and grander moods.   Here, in nature herself, is "difficult beauty."

Nor is it a problem primarily of aesthetic form, although it is true that "difficult beauty" often appears inharmonious, dis-

---

[1] B. Bosanquet, *Three Lectures on Aesthetic*, London, 1915, Lecture III.
[2] DeWitt H. Parker, *Principles of Aesthetics*, New York, 1920. *The Analysis of Art*, New Haven, 1926.

proportionate, and without rhythmic quality. For example, the grotesque may seem wildly disproportionate; the tragic, inharmonious; the sublime, without definite pattern. Nothing of aesthetic value, however, can be wholly without aesthetic form. It has been pointed out that aesthetic form is that definition of a complex object which makes possible the perceptual grasp of the object. It is impossible to hold that the essential nature of "difficult beauty" is that the object having this kind of beauty be without aesthetic form or even deficient in it. To the degree that it is without or deficient in form, it would be without or deficient in value, for the form is a necessary (though not the sufficient) condition for the existence of the value. If the grotesque seems disproportionate and without form, it is only because it has form to which we are not accustomed. To define "difficult beauty" by reference to forms to which one is not accustomed is to make the unwarranted assumption that it is "natural" for customary forms to give us pleasure and "not natural" for that which is unusual to yield pleasure. Such an assumption explains nothing.

Only that object which involves complexities that are wholly beyond the grasp of the perceptual sensibility can be called without pattern and without rhythm. It may be that the forms of "difficult beauty" are such as involve complexities which are beyond the grasp of undeveloped sensibilities. Persons who have these undeveloped sensibilities are apt to call the forms inharmonious and disproportionate, but these forms are not beyond the powers of apprehension of other sensibilities. If they were, they not only would not have "difficult beauty," but would have no kind of aesthetic value whatever. The very statement of the problem of "difficult beauty," however, recognizes that they are of aesthetic value. When they are called inharmonious and disproportionate, only one of two things can be meant: either the form which they display is not that to which most persons are accustomed, or the form is too complex for undeveloped sensibilities to grasp. These alternatives may, in the last analysis, mean the same thing. What seems relatively without form to some individuals may not seem so to others. This is partly dependent upon a standard of taste, for one's powers of apprehension are not independent of his habits of perception.

The problem of "difficult beauty" is only partly a problem of aesthetic values. Actual value is a function of the apprehension of an individual. If there is no actual apprehension, there is no actual value, but in any given case it is possible that there would be apprehension of value if an aesthetic attitude were taken. In this situation, it is accurate to speak of potential values. There may be a high degree of potential value in any particular case of "difficult beauty"; there may be a greater potentiality than in a given case of "easy beauty." An object of great potential value may not appeal to a wide audience, because it is only imperfectly grasped by weak sensibilities. When the sensibility is more adequate and the grasp is more complete, however, a more complex object will yield more pleasure, for more activity is involved in its grasp. The problem of "difficult beauty," then becomes the question of whether or not the potential values are actually realized.

3.

Definition of the problem. It is evident that the problem of "difficult beauty" is a problem of appreciation. There is no essential difference either in aesthetic form or in aesthetic value between "difficult beauty" and any other kind of beauty. Any view holding that there is is based upon a mimetic or a representative theory of art, whether such theory is explicit or implicit, recognized or unrecognized. The "difficulty" grows out of the fact that sometimes art uses subject matter which is unpleasant in some context of real life or the empirical world. If it is the function of art to imitate or to represent the situations of the real world, art is portraying something which is, in its original nature, unpleasant. Thus there arises the problem of how the representation of an unpleasant thing becomes pleasant. All this follows from the representative theory of art; but if the representative theory of art is seen to be inadequate, and if the meaning of the term "aesthetic" is thoroughly understood, there is no intrinsic reason why "the forms of the most ignoble animals, and of dead bodies" should be aesthetically repellent, while the forms of noble animals and live bodies are not. There may be plenty of reason, however, why they are morally or practically or sentimentally repellent. "Ignoble" is a term of moral reproach. "Death" is the name of a biological condition. Neither is a term of primary aesthetic meaning.

"Difficult beauty" is positive aesthetic value whose appreciation is made difficult by the intrusion of nonaesthetic attitudes. Such attitudes are concerned with nonaesthetic data. Any phenomenon may have nonaesthetic aspects that are unpleasant even though the apprehension of the aesthetic aspects may be pleasant; and this is the case when there is "difficult beauty." The difficulty is caused by aspects which are unpleasant to the moral or practical or intellectual or some other nonaesthetic attitude. This unpleasantness tends to prohibit or to inhibit or destroy the aesthetic attitude, and so to hinder the appreciation of aesthetic value.

4.

Illustration from tragedy. To take an example, tragic drama deals with situations that are morally unpleasant. Drama deals with the conditions and situations of living. Most persons are accustomed to take a moral attitude toward life. This is necessary in practice, because acting, doing, and behaving are indispensable to life. Tragedy deals with pain and suffering and defeat, and, consistent with biological preservation, moralism denies, evades, or abhors pain and suffering and defeat. The fact that situations which are morally unpleasant produce aesthetic pleasure is what seems to be the "difficulty," but it is not a difficulty arising from the fundamental nature of the aesthetic value. It is a difficulty of appreciation caused by the intrusion of the moral attitude. Just because the situation is unpleasant to the moral attitude is no reason why it should be unpleasant to the aesthetic attitude. The unpleasantness is not something which inheres in the nature of the situation; it is a function of the moral attitude, and the aesthetic attitude is not the moral attitude; it is the very inversion of the moral attitude.

Not only the moral attitude stands in the way of an appreciation of tragedy, but the intellectual sensibility is also apt to intrude. Tragic drama is usually profound and its portrayal is subtle. The tragic artist sees and portrays aesthetic realities that are far beyond those evident to the superficial observer. The intellect which cannot easily and without effort grasp the situations with which tragic drama deals will intrude on the aesthetic attitude. Drama is a very mixed form of art. There are in it many aspects other than the perceptual aspects. If a nonaesthetic aspect commands the attention and attitude of the observer, then the appreciation of aesthetic value is impossible. For instance, if an auditor listening to a drama in the English language understands English so imperfectly that his whole attention is directed toward getting the words and sentences, his appreciation is inhibited thereby. The understanding of the language is an intellectual matter, but a lack of understanding will obviously hinder appreciation of aesthetic value in an art so mixed as poetry or drama. The understanding must be so fluent that it can be exercised without being the object of attention. If it is, the attention can be directed toward the perceptual aspects of whatever is in hand, that is, the aesthetic attitude may be taken and aesthetic value apprehended. In tragic drama, if the complexity of the situations baffles the intellect of the auditor, the aesthetic attitude will be rendered impossible and the appreciation of tragedy difficult, but if the situations can be grasped intellectually without directing attention especially toward them, the aesthetic values can become apparent.

The aesthetic value of tragedy, or of all "difficult beauty" in general, does not need for its explanation the formulation of any principles other than those necessary for the explanation of all aesthetic value. In other words, an especial "theory of tragedy" is unnecessary in aesthetics. A lack of developed or sensitive taste causes the intrusion of attitudes other than the aesthetic, which inhibit the appreciation of the tragic, the sublime, the grotesque, and so forth. If there is a lack of sensitiveness, and if the art is profound, most of the aesthetic values in it will go unrealized. The habitual standard of taste can never truly appreciate what is profound. Much that seems grotesque is so only because it is not what one is accustomed to see. The background for the appreciation of tragedy must be broad and taste must be developed in order that the derived values potential in the situation can be realized. With an insufficiently developed sensitiveness, the appreciation will remain "difficult."

5.

The problem of ugliness. "Difficult beauty" is not ugliness, nor has it much to do with ugliness, but the reasons why "difficult beauty" has seemed to offer such a stubborn problem for aesthetics center in the unfortunate use of the term "beauty" in aesthetic theory.[2] It is likewise the case that, when the term "beauty" is used to denote the central conception of aesthetics, the problem of ugliness is concealed. It seems apparent that the ugly is that which is not beautiful, and one is tempted to let it go at that. When one does not allow himself to be confused by words, however, and sees that the central conception of aesthetics is a certain kind of value, then it becomes evident that the ugly is not an absolute lack of aesthetic value, but is the disvalue. Only that of which perceptual grasp in any degree is impossible or toward which an aesthetic attitude could never be taken would lack all potential aesthetic value. Aesthetics would have no concern with such objects, if there were any.

Actual aesthetic value is dependent upon the aesthetic attitude. If one is not in the aesthetic attitude, but in the moral or intellectual or practical or some other attitude, he is not apprehending aesthetic value. That which he is apprehending is not ugliness: that which is moral or practical is not ugly because it is not aesthetic. Ugliness is something apprehended in the aesthetic attitude; hence, it is incumbent upon aesthetic theory to discover what the term "ugliness" means when it is used more or less accurately. It was not until the nineteenth century that thinkers explicitly recognized this. Solger, a contemporary of Hegel, attacked the problem with insight, although his attempted solution is hardly adequate because it is dependent upon his general intellectualistic theory of beauty. Rosenkranz, a follower of Hegel, published an *Aesthetic of Ugliness* in 1853. In contemporary times, Professor Langfeld,

---

[2] See above, Chapter VI, Section 7.

with a reference to Lipps, defines aesthetics as "the science of beauty and ugliness." [3]   The whole course of the development of this tendency in the history of aesthetics indicates that unless aesthetics is the study of two different subjects, "ugliness" and "beauty" are relative to each other, and are the opposite ends of a scale of values.

The uncritical view that ugliness, as the opposite of beauty, is not an especial concern of aesthetic theory, often assumes that ugliness is a lack of aesthetic form.   Ugliness could not mean an absolute lack of aesthetic form, for it is not apparent what an absolute lack of aesthetic form itself could mean.   All complex perceptual data must be organized in some way or other, and an absolute lack of aesthetic form then would mean a lack of all that is perceptual, that is, aesthetic in any sense of the term.   If ugliness be taken to mean a relative lack of aesthetic form, it must be pointed out again, as it was in Section 2 of the present chapter, that a relative lack of rhythm, pattern, proportion, or balance may mean either a rhythm, pattern, proportion, or balance to which the observer is not accustomed, or a greater degree of complexity than he can grasp.   The word "ugliness" is often used uncritically and naively in common speech to describe objects which have rhythms and patterns to which one is not accustomed.   This meaning of the word is not satisfactory, as it would make ugliness relative to an habitual standard of taste.

---

[3] For further references see Bosanquet, *History of Aesthetic,* London, 1910, pp. 396–401.   H. S. Langfeld, *The Aesthetic Attitude,* New York, 1920, p. 34.

6.

Bosanquet's theory of ugliness. A more satisfactory explanation of ugliness is that given by Bosanquet in the third of his *Three Lectures on Aesthetic.*[4] He says, on page 103, "if the ugly is the unaesthetic, well then it is not aesthetic at all, and we are not concerned with it." Bosanquet is concerned with it, however, and finds a meaning for it other than the unaesthetic. He says that in any object judged to be ugly there must be some aesthetic appeal: some element which suggests that there may be aesthetic values in the object. Suppose one portion of it to be a malformation destroying the aesthetic effect of the whole. Bosanquet says the malformation in this case may well be called ugly. In this sense, the ugly is that part of a possible aesthetic whole that does not fulfill the expectation of the aesthetic sensibility concerning the whole. There is something in the object which awakens the aesthetic interest, and awakens at the same time an expectation of the way in which that interest will be satisfied; but something else in the object violently disappoints this expectation. Ugliness is the disappointment of the aesthetic sensibility that is aroused but not gratified. Ugliness, for this definition, is the thwarted expectation of beauty.

This solution of the problem of ugliness is due to Solger. "If anything is to be recognized as the opposite of the beautiful, the same thing must be looked for that is looked for in the

---

[4] Bosanquet, *Three Lectures on Aesthetic*, London, 1915.

beautiful, and the opposite found." [5]   Bosanquet's own example is that the silky ear of a dachshund on the head of a person would rightly be considered ugly; but looked at by itself or on the head of a dachshund, it is beautiful.   With this conception, to say that a whole was in itself ugly—insuperably ugly— would be meaningless.

7.

Ugliness is aesthetic disvalue.   This explanation of ugliness is not wholly satisfactory, for it gives ugliness meaning relative only to a standard of taste.   What an individual looks for in any aesthetic object is determined by his standard of taste. That the ear of a dachshund is not acceptable on the head of a person can be accounted for only by the fact that one is not accustomed to see it there.   If ugliness is a thwarted expectation of beauty, then both beauty and ugliness are relative to a standard of taste.   In this case, the whole study of aesthetics is in an impasse, for a standard of taste can be explained only after aesthetic values have been defined.   Beauty and ugliness are aesthetic values; hence, the person who makes them dependent upon a standard of taste is involved in a vicious circle.

This is an excellent example of the confusions which are introduced into aesthetics by the use of the term "beauty" as a technical term covering the whole of aesthetic value.   "Beauty" may be the common name for aesthetic value, but in actual speech it is used to denote only positive values, and only relatively high degrees of positive values at that.   Ugliness is con-

---

[5] Quoted from Solger's *Vorlesungen über Aesthetic*, p. 101, by Bosanquet, *History of Aesthetic*, p. 396.

ceived to be the antithesis of beauty; but if beauty denotes all aesthetic value, and if ugliness is its antithesis, then ugliness is the complete opposite of, or absolute lack of, aesthetic value. This kind of a view displays hopeless confusion. It is due to the use of the term "value" in one sentence in a positive sense and in the next sentence in a generic sense, without distinguishing between them.

There are positive and negative aesthetic values. These differ from each other according to the evaluating factor. "Beauty" is one of the common names for the positive value. "Ugliness" is the common name for the negative value, that is, the disvalue. In actual speech, it may be used with any one of a number of different shades of meaning; hence it is no more satisfactory technical terminology than is "beauty." As far as a consideration of ugliness is of moment to aesthetic theory, it must be understood as the negative value or aesthetic disvalue. It is the lower end of the scale of evaluation for all aesthetic values.

The difference between negative and positive values can be understood only after an evaluating factor has been introduced for the measure of values. The relation between negative and positive values depends upon this evaluating factor. The evaluating factor for aesthetic value is pleasure in the aesthetic attitude. Positive aesthetic value is experienced when one takes pleasure in the apprehension of the perceptual aspects of phenomena. If, for any reason whatever, one is concerned with the perceptual aspects of phenomena, and the apprehension of them gives rise, not to pleasure, but to displeasure, then he is experiencing the disvalue or ugliness.

It makes no difference what has led one to take the aesthetic attitude. The cause of taking the attitude is irrelevant; what is important is the result. If, for no matter what reason, one takes the aesthetic attitude, and displeasure results, the negative value has been apprehended. There may be something in the perceptual appearance of the object which, giving promise of fulfilling interest, calls forth the attitude. This is the only case accounted for by Bosanquet's theory. The negative value is apprehended, however, when there is displeasure in the aesthetic attitude, even though one's attention has been called to the perceptual appearance of the object by some extraneous circumstance such as the explicit words of another. The aesthetic attitude may have been elicited by irrelevant causes, but if displeasure results, the observer has experienced ugliness.

Neither does it in the least matter what has caused the displeasure, as long as that displeasure has come in the aesthetic attitude. If displeasure is present when attention is directed wholly toward the data of perceptual intuition, that is enough. One may experience unpleasantness because of inadequate powers of perception. Or he may experience unpleasantness because the structure of the object is too complex for perception (even though highly trained) to grasp. In this case, ugliness is dependent upon a relative lack of aesthetic form. Or he may experience unpleasantness because of inability to discriminate between aesthetic values (or, in this case, disvalues) and other values (or disvalues). What many persons call ugly is, instead, only that of which they morally disapprove. In this case, ugliness is a function of aesthetic vulgarity and is closely allied to the sensitiveness of taste of the individual. In other cases, the unpleasantness that arises in the aesthetic attitude might result merely from a peculiarity in the education of the taste of the individual.

In none of these cases is ugliness anything absolute. It is always relative to the individual. Of course, there is no such thing as "insuperable ugliness," if by this phrase is meant absolute ugliness. There may be insuperable ugliness if the phrase be taken to mean that no one can be expected to apprehend the perceptual aspects of the object with pleasure: if it means that there is nothing pleasant to see or hear even when a person sees or hears all there is or all that is possible. If, in the criticism of art, one can find reason for supposing that there are only disvalues potential in an object, then that object cannot be judged to be a successful work of art; but if one finds that an object is ugly, and the displeasure is to be explained by reference to aesthetic vulgarity or by a peculiarity of his taste, the object cannot be evaluated as a poor work of art. It is probable that today, in the cases of most persons who judge certain tendencies in modern art to be ugly, the judgment is merely an expression of their taste. Hence, it may be only a reflection of the incapacity of the individual to appreciate a wide assortment of aesthetic values—only a measure of his insensibility.

If one experiences ugliness, the unpleasantness may actually destroy the aesthetic attitude. If it becomes great, it is almost bound to do so, for unpleasantness is the affective tone of the tendency to avoid. Even though it destroy the aesthetic attitude, the negative value has been apprehended when displeasure has been experienced in the aesthetic attitude. That unpleasantness does work effectively to destroy the aesthetic attitude is the explanation of the fact that people so often become inured to ugliness in their everyday surroundings, and oblivious of it.

In the present study, the term "aesthetic value" is used either in its generic sense to denote both positive and negative values, or to denote only positive values. It is always clear from the context whether the broad generic sense or the more narrow positive sense is meant. Whenever the *negative* value is intended, it is necessary explicitly to indicate it. For example, when it is said that aesthetic value is value apprehended in the perceptual aspects of phenomena, it is clear that the generic sense is intended. When it is said that aesthetic value is apprehended when one experiences pleasure in perceptual grasp, it is clear that this is the definition of the positive value. Displeasure in perception is the sign of the disvalue. When the term is used in the definition of art, the positive value is meant. The positive and negative values are relative to each other and cannot be fully understood except in relation to each other. Pleasure, the evaluating factor for the measure of values, determines their relation.

CHAPTER XI

Applied Aesthetics

1.

The criticism of art is applied aesthetics. The field of applied aesthetics is much more extensive than it is possible to delineate in a detailed way within the limits of a single chapter. In addition to this, the purpose of the present study is to give the essentials of an aesthetic theory, and this purpose may be accomplished without going into the details of applications. It is true, however, that any theory that does not work in application is a poor theory. Hence, it is good to make a rapid survey of the field of applied aesthetics and see how the present theory works in application.

The criticism of art is, perhaps, the most important application of theoretic aesthetics. The criticism of art is not appreciation, but is evaluation. It is true that criticism is usually not worth much unless it is based upon appreciation, but it goes beyond appreciation. As evaluative, criticism is intellectual. One may be able to apprehend a high degree of aesthetic value without being able to explain in intellectual terms exactly why he does so; he may be able to see value without being able to point it out. The critic of art, however, must be able to say why he apprehends value and must be able to point it out. Thus, art criticism is always applied aesthetics even though the critic be not aware of it or even though he deny it. He must know what aesthetic values are, must be able to evaluate a work of art as art, and be able to give sufficient reasons for his evaluation. His task may include more than this, but whatever else he does, unless he accomplishes this, he is not a critic of art.

The first task of the critic is to point out the aesthetic values potential in any work of art. A work is art to the degree of adequacy with which it conveys aesthetic values. The apprehension of these values is based on perception, and it is not always easy to perceive all there is to be perceived in a complex situation. The critic should be able to point out what there is to be perceived. His own powers of perception should be acute and trained, his taste should be cultivated to a high standard, and he must know enough about the kind of art criticized to be able to look for and to find the values potential in it. As the values potential in the work of art are dependent upon what there is to be perceived in it, the critic directs attention to the perceptual aspects of the art. What he has pointed out once, the observer may be able to see for himself another time.

An exaggerated example of the task of the critic, and the result of this task upon the observer, can be found in a consideration of a kind of line puzzle that often amuses children. The very exaggeration of this case is illustrative, because it brings out so clearly the effect of pointing out what there is to see. The puzzle is an intricate line design with directions something to this effect: "Hidden in this picture are four funny faces; find them." If the design is skillfully made, one rarely can see the faces at once. After a careful perusal, he may be able to see them. And when he does succeed in finding them, or if someone points them out to him, he cannot look at the picture again without these faces staring at him. There they are, and he cannot fail to see them or avoid seeing them any more.

The one who points out the faces is the ancestor of the art critic. In the work of art, if it is at all profound, there are many perceptual aspects that the casual observer does not see at once. It is the business of the critic to point them out and make him see them. After having had his attention effectively called to them, the observer cannot fail to see them, and if there is pleasure in the perception, he is apprehending aesthetic value. The critic must be able to make the blind see and the deaf hear. The critic must discern more than the ordinary person, and then must be able to show him what he did not see or hear in such a way as to enable him to see or to hear it.

The task of the critic might not be directed wholly toward increasing the appreciation of the observer, however. An observer may think that a given work is art or is beautiful, but the critic might be able to point out that his pleasure really lies in the nonaesthetic aspects of the object. In the first chapter of the present study, the situation was described in which a person supposes a certain elaborate piece of interior architecture or a vivid chromolithograph to be beautiful.[1]   In the cases cited, the pleasure was to be found not so much in the aesthetic aspects of the object as in the nonaesthetic aspects.   Perhaps the cases cited were too exaggerated to be taken as examples of opportunity for art criticism, but the very exaggeration is illustrative.   If there is any occasion for criticism, the critic can point out that sentimentalized patriotism is not an appreciation of aesthetic value, nor is mouth-watering beauty.

In further pursuance of his negative task, the critic may point out that all the apparent values in any work of art are only superficial, and that the appeal of the work is candidly to some superficial character of perceptual grasp.   He may find values only suggested, and not displayed.   By means of his knowledge of the art under question and the history of art, and by means of a comparison of the present work with other works, he may be able to show a comparative poverty of value.   These considerations make up the negative or "destructive" side of the critic's task.   Criticism, being evaluative judgment, involves comparison.   Thus there may be reference to aesthetic values other than those in the work under consideration.   Hence the work under consideration may be judged to be *better* or *worse*.

The task of the critic goes beyond pointing out the presence or comparative absence of aesthetic values.   In fact, it goes beyond the purely aesthetic aspect of the work of art.   He must be aware of the nonaesthetic aspects of the work and be able to deal with them.   Any given work of art is much more than

---

[1] See above, pp. 10–11.

a conveyance for aesthetic values. It may mean something, or teach a moral lesson, or have other aspects in addition to the aesthetic. As sources of derived values, the other aspects may be important either when considered by themselves or when considered in their bearing upon the apprehension of aesthetic values in the work. The critic can perform a great service to appreciation by giving the beholder a background for these derived values. Or, the nonaesthetic aspects of a work of art may effectively hinder the apprehension of the aesthetic values that it conveys, and the critic, when he points out the reasons for the hindrance, clarifies appreciation.

The critic must be able to judge whether or not the subject matter of the work of art under consideration is apt to produce displeasure when regarded from the standpoint of nonaesthetic attitudes. He must be able to judge whether or not this is apt to affect the apprehension of aesthetic values, and if so, under what conditions. He must be able to help the observer to discriminate between aesthetic and nonaesthetic values. He must guard the observer against aesthetic vulgarity. The most dangerously inadequate of all critics is he who falls into some confusion and displays some kind of aesthetic vulgarity himself. Many persons consider the critic an "authority," and take his judgment at its face value; but, of course, he is no authority in an absolute sense, and his judgment is always liable to error. There are no "authorities" in aesthetic appreciation. The critic may be able to point out something that he sees, but he cannot make the observer see it if the observer cannot. Nor can the observer be led to see it merely by "taking the critic as an authority." All genuine judgments of taste are individual.

Criticism may exert an important influence in the formation

of a standard of taste. Many of the habits of perception of most persons are molded by criticism, either "official" or "unofficial" criticism: that is, either supposedly expert or professional criticism, or the expressed preferences of one's associates. The training of the powers of perception and of discrimination is an important element in the formation of a standard of taste. Criticism, in pointing out what to see, forms habits of perception in the observer: the observer looks for similar things in similar situations. Criticism determines to a large extent what one looks for in a work of art. Criticism can help one attain even the highest level of taste by acquainting him with some of the elementary methods of technique of the kind of art under consideration, thus enhancing the apprehension of derived aesthetic values. In this case, however, the critic must again be very careful not to engender aesthetic vulgarity instead of developing taste. No critic can be competent to this task in whose mind is the slightest confusion concerning the nature of aesthetic values.

2.

The task of criticism. Much of the actual criticism that one comes across today may be classified under one of two heads: it may be called either "impressionistic" criticism or "academic" criticism. Neither of these kinds is adequate to the critic's task. Impressionistic criticism is "a mere recording of certain sensations"; [2] that is, the critic contemplates the work of art and

---

[2] Roger Fry, *Vision and Design*, London, 1920, p. 188.

records his impressions of it. The success of such criticism depends upon the creation of another work of art, this time literary art, to embody in a new form something like the values of the original work, and hence to enable one to apprehend the values of the original. Aesthetic values are not easily transferable from one medium to another, however. One may apprehend the values of the piece of literary art, but still be insensible to the values in the original work that is being criticized if this is, say, a piece of music or of sculpture or of architecture. If this impressionistic criticism performs any function at all in relation to the first work of art, it is merely in leading one to observe the work carefully and sympathetically. As a new piece of art, the so-called criticism must stand on its own merits.

Academic criticism criticizes according to rule. Hence it is very apt to be either a criticism of technique, or historical criticism, or both, and as such it is inadequate. The vehicle for the conveyance of aesthetic value can be constructed according to rule, but the vision of value comes according to no rule. Neither can it be measured by a rule. Technique is the exercise of the rules of construction of the vehicle, and a criticism of technique may be only the criticism of a vehicle empty of values. This is not criticism of art, for the art of the work depends upon its conveyance of values. Furthermore, rules are based on that which is established; hence academic criticism is inhospitable and blind to values conveyed by new forms and new methods of technique. All historical criticism is likewise apt to be hidebound, for its standards are dependent upon what has been done and recognized in the past.

To be adequate to his task, the critic should be thoroughly acquainted with the nature of aesthetic value and with the conditions of its apprehension. He must know both the history and the general methods of technique of the art that he is criticizing. He must know these in order to have attained to the highest level of taste and to be able to point out comparative values and lack of values. Of course, the knowledge alone will not ensure that he has attained to the highest level of taste. In order to be able to point out to others what they might not see otherwise, he must be sensitive to aesthetic values of the kind with which he is dealing; and he must have a high degree of discrimination in order to avoid aesthetic vulgarity. All of this ability and preparation is applied to each separate work of art which he must evaluate, and its adequacy in conveying aesthetic values and its effect upon the nonaesthetic attitudes of the observer must be carefully estimated.

All critical judgments, in the last analysis, go back to the individual work of art, but criticism can be general to any desired degree. There can be criticism of a group of works of art that are similar to each other, such as a criticism of Elizabethan drama; or of larger subdivisions, such as a criticism of dramatic art in general; or of a main division of art, such as a critical study of literature. As the criticism of art becomes more general, it approaches a critical philosophy of art.

3.

The philosophy of art. Much of the usual philosophy of art is applied aesthetics. One especial field for such application lies in the consideration of the materials, techniques, and methods of portrayal of the several arts. For example, painting makes use of color and line, and by the use of these suggests a third dimension and texture. Sculpture and architecture use actual three-dimensional volume and actual texture. The materials of music are tones and noises; the materials of literature are sounds and words; the materials of the dance are bodily movements. Many interesting problems arise in the consideration of the natures of these materials, of the way that structures may be built from them, and of the way that these formal structures embody aesthetic values. Rhythm is the basic principle of aesthetic form in the temporal arts such as music, poetry, and the dance. Proportion and balance are the more characteristic principles of form in the spatial arts. All such questions as these are interesting and worthy of full analysis, but they are questions of applied aesthetics, not strictly of theoretic aesthetics.

A study of the subject matters of the various arts is also a field for applied aesthetics. Is the best subject matter for painting abstract or representative? What kind of subject matter can architecture and music best portray? Subject matters can be classified as abstract, descriptive, narrative, dramatic, emotional, and in other ways. Much can be determined about the way that each kind of art uses these different kinds of subject matter, which arts handle which kinds with the greatest degree of success, and how aesthetic values are embodied in each kind.

Any art may portray subject matter which is not usual or characteristic to it: it may portray a subject matter which seems better fitted to the medium of some other kind of art. This fact raises an important question for applied aesthetics: Is it a legitimate point of evaluation to consider whether or not a certain work of art is attempting to do what can better be done in another medium? This is a specific case of the more general problem of the delimitation of the arts. It is apparent on the basis of the theory of aesthetics given in the present study that the limitation of each art to its definition in terms of materials and technique does not offer any principle of evaluation. The differences between the arts are largely a matter of traditional growth. If any art oversteps its accustomed material, this does not necessarily make it bad art, nor does it make it good art. Art can be evaluated only in terms of its adequacy in conveyance of aesthetic values. If a picture tells a story, or if a piece of music is descriptive, that fact may either add to or detract from its value. It can detract only in case the story distracts the attention from the aesthetic values that can best be conveyed by painting, or if the program draws attention from the aesthetic value of the music. These values are largely formal values, and if the painting or the music has none of them in the first place, it is a poor piece of art to begin with, and the fact that it tells a story cannot overcome or mitigate the deficiency.

Some kinds of art are frankly combined arts, such as the song, opera, drama, and so forth. Whether the dance is considered, a combined art depends upon whether music is regarded as an integral part of it or only as an accompaniment. The fact that these arts are combined does not necessarily make them any better or any worse. The problems of technique may be made very difficult by the combination; hence it might not be expected that the combined arts will be successful, but this offers no principle of evaluation. The only principle of evaluation is the adequacy of conveyance of aesthetic value.

Inquiry into the methods of portrayal, technique, and subject matter within any one art gives rise to the distinctions known to criticism as romanticism, realism, classicism, and so forth. At present there is no settled terminology for criticism here: literary criticism usually uses the distinction between realism and naturalism in one way, and the criticism of painting usually uses it in the diametrically opposite way. The actual terminology used is of minor importance as long as the distinctions are clear, and the distinctions can be clear only in case the theory behind them is clear. The difference between romanticism and realism on the one hand, and between realism and naturalism on the other, can be made clear only by an application of the theory of art. When it is understood that the work of art is a product of the vision of the artist and his choice of technique and method of portrayal, romanticism can be distinguished from realism by referring to the emotional quality of the vision of the artist. Realism can be distinguished from naturalism by referring to the selection used in the method of portrayal.

4.

The philistine and puritan condemnation of art. The field of aesthetics comes into contact with the fields of other interests, and this contact often engenders conflicts. Two characteristic condemnations of art arise from such conflicts: the philistine condemns art on economic grounds, and the puritan condemns it on moral grounds. The views of both the philistine and the puritan are illustrative of some knotty practical problems whose solution falls within the province of applied aesthetics. Is the production of all would-be art economically justified; and is it not possible for art to display such a character as must be morally condemned? Such questions can never be solved with even a semblance of adequacy except on the basis of a clear understanding of aesthetic theory.

For example, the philistine calls art a useless and wasteful luxury. His wrath may be directed mainly against the production of art and its costly preservation. Perhaps he calls the artist a parasite on society; or he decries the wastefulness of the preservation of natural beauty. If nature may be put to practical use, even though that use involves the destruction of superb scenic beauty, the beauty is, in the United States, usually ruthlessly sacrificed, and the philistine is well pleased. Many of our cities and towns are blots on an already dull landscape—aesthetic atrocities which bespeak our insensibility to appearance. To make them more beautiful would entail an outlay that the philistine considers a waste, and hence not justified. Is or is not the philistine, in making these judgments, displaying an intelligent attitude? Even though his attitude may be judged to be not very intelligent, there are cases when one has to decide whether to sacrifice beauty or to disregard the economic demands of the moment. Wherever these come into conflict, a choice must be made. The solution of this problem in any particular case is a practical matter, but requires both a knowledge of economic principles and an understanding of the principles of aesthetics. One must know what aesthetic value is, where it may be found, and its relation to his total experience. Aesthetic appreciation is close to the basis of all experience, for it depends on perceiving what there is to be perceived. Hence, any economic policy that condemns it as a useless luxury is not dealing adequately with experience.

The puritan condemns art, not on economic grounds, but on moral grounds. His disapproval of art and his fear of an over-emphasis on the appreciation of beauty is due primarily to the fact that pleasure is a concomitant of aesthetic value, and the puritan is profoundly suspicious of pleasure. The endeavor to answer the puritan's criticism has led sometimes to an attempt to show that pleasure is not an essential of the aesthetic experience, and sometimes to an attempt to show that even if it is, it is justified because of the Truth and Goodness of Beauty. It is clear in the light of the present study that the first attempt is hopeless and the second is irrelevant. Pleasure not only always accompanies the apprehension of aesthetic value but is its evaluating factor. Hence, if the puritan is suspicious of pleasure, he might well be suspicious of aesthetic value. The puritan criticism of art is borne out, but the puritan standard of morality is put in question.

Of course, the solution of the problem entailed in the puritan condemnation of art requires a thorough knowledge of ethical principles as well as aesthetic principles. Hence, its solution lies beyond the scope of the present study, but it is plain that the puritan attitude is bound up with an ascetic theory of morality. Furthermore, the puritan condemnation of the appreciation of aesthetic value completely misunderstands the relation between sensuous pleasure and aesthetic pleasure. If the present study is correct as to the relation between these two, a suspicion of sensuous pleasure (which is all the puritan is usually concerned with) does not carry with it any sweeping generalization about aesthetic value. The puritan condemnation does not understand the conditions of the aesthetic attitude. Of course, even if it did, it might look upon this attitude with disfavor because of its rigoristic code of morality. This again would call into question the adequacy of that code.

5.

The censorship of art. The problem of censorship of art involves much more than the puritan suspicion of art. Censorship is often undertaken under the domination of or even the direct control of a puritan influence, but a satisfactory solution of the problem is not to be attained from the standpoint of the puritan alone. Both theoretical and practical questions of good government and of education are pertinent to the solution. For example, art, especially literary art, may be used for propaganda purposes. Literature, being a very mixed art, has many aspects other than aesthetic, and it is possible that, even though the aesthetic value of any given work may be great, its other aspects are such that it must be condemned on political grounds or moral grounds. Where such a conflict arises, a nice choice must be made in every particular case. Some aesthetic values must be lost or negative values of another kind will become apparent. No *a priori* rule can be laid down concerning the nature of the choice in every instance. If the aesthetic values are great and the nonaesthetic disvalues are unimportant, a choice against censorship is indicated. If the disvalues are preponderant and important, they may tip the balance and indicate the desirability of censorship. To assume, however, as some of the advocates of censorship seem to assume, that aesthetic values are always of little importance, and therefore that censorship is desirable wherever nonaesthetic disvalues are apparent, is to show utter ignorance concerning the relation between aesthetic and nonaesthetic values and concerning the nature of the aesthetic experience.

It is possible for obscene literature or pornographic painting to show a high degree of material and formal aesthetic value. In this case the problem of censorship is much more easily solved if one understands the conditions of the aesthetic attitude and the dependence of aesthetic value upon this attitude. Censorship of this kind of art may be justified because it is rare for such aesthetic values as are potential in the art to be realized. Sexual interest is more impelling than the aesthetic; hence, this interest, or the moral interest dependent upon it, is almost sure to intrude and render the aesthetic attitude impossible. The sexual interest might be either positive or negative; that is, it might display itself either as lasciviousness or as disgust and condemnation; but in either case it has displaced the aesthetic attitude. Consequently, the aesthetic aspect of that which is obscene or pornographic is rarely predominant, and censorship is not so much condemning art as it is condemning obscenity. It may be necessary to condemn obscenity in order to preserve the nervous health of the individual and of society.

The actions of men, especially those undertaken *en masse,* are controlled by emotion more than by any other motive force. Art has great power to evoke and to sway emotions. As was pointed out above,[3] the pleasure of emotional states can become an incidental part of the evaluating factor for aesthetic value, but this is subject to the conditions of the aesthetic attitude. When a work of art moves men to act and to do, the aesthetic attitude is no longer manifest. Thus, as was the case in art condemned for reasons of sex morality, to condemn a piece of propaganda art is not always primarily to condemn art. If its aspect as propaganda overshadows its aesthetic aspect, one is condemning what is not primarily art when he attempts to censor it.

Another point to consider when one attacks the problem of censorship is that actual attempts at censorship often result in aggravating the conditions they are supposed to correct. Censorship serves to call attention to the works of art that are condemned, and thus to center an artificial interest in them. When the aesthetic values in a disputed work are predominant, the nonaesthetic disvalues might be lost to sight and disappear if the censor did not call attention to them. His disapproval usually ensures that the wrong persons will get hold of the work,

---

[3] See above, Chapter VI, Section 6.

that is, those persons who, because of the nature of their taste, will be more apt to see the nonaesthetic aspects and less apt to appreciate the aesthetic values. As long as a work is predominantly a work of art—a successful vehicle for the conveyance of aesthetic values—the nonaesthetic disvalues in it probably are best censored by ignoring them. Even if it is not predominantly a work of art, the possibility still remains that the best way of censoring it is to ignore it. If positive censorship is attempted, it must be thorough, or it will not accomplish its aim.

All of these considerations are, in the broadest sense, moral, and it is usually presumed that the problem of censorship is wholly, or at least primarily, a moral problem. This presumption is based upon an utter lack of understanding of the nature of aesthetic value and of the relation between aesthetic and moral value. It assumes implicitly or explicitly that moral values are higher than aesthetic values and exercise a sanction over them; that moral values somehow include aesthetic values. In order to define aesthetic values, however, it is necessary to distinguish them clearly from moral values; they cannot be subsumed under moral values. Aesthetic value is intrinsic; hence could not be dependent upon moral value for its essential nature. On the other hand, most moral values are instrumental. An instrumental value is valuable only because it leads toward some intrinsic value. Aesthetic value is the intrinsic value *par excellence*. Hence, it is possible that the connection between moral and aesthetic values is exactly opposite to that presumed by the usual attitude toward the problem of censorship.

6.

Aesthetics and epistemology. All knowledge is based upon the aesthetic experience: aesthetic in the sense of being the experience of perceptual intuition. Of course this does not mean that all knowledge is based on the apprehension of aesthetic value. The aesthetic experience involves the apprehension of positive value only when interest is centered in the data of perceptual intuition in their own nature and when pleasure is taken in the apprehension of these data. If there is any such thing as aesthetic value, it is experienced as a part of the aesthetic experience conceived in the broadest manner possible as perceptual intuition. It has been pointed out above that perception of fact is based upon perceptual intuition,[4] but in the perception of fact the interest is centered in something other than the perceptual aspect of the object considered in its own nature; hence no apprehension of aesthetic value ensues. Nevertheless, the aesthetic basis of all experience is present even though it is immediately transcended. Concepts are present in the perception of fact; it is a cognitive act. Concepts are incipient in perceptual intuition in the sense that perceptual intuition becomes the perception of fact if the attitude changes.

The perceptual (aesthetic) element seems to be present in all knowledge whatsoever, no matter how "abstract." Psychology has been unsuccessful in the attempt to find "imageless thought." Even the knowledge of abstract relations is based

---

[4] See above, Chapter III, Section 4.

on particular perceptions of fact. Through the processes of analysis, abstraction, and generalization, mathematics may seem to get far from the realms of concrete reality, but back at the foundations of the most abstruse mathematical knowledge can be found the aesthetic data from which the original generalizations were made. And even the most highly generalized mathematical ideas have their symbols and are dealt with by means of their symbols. These symbols are aesthetic data.

Aesthetics may be looked at from either of two angles: either from the viewpoint of epistemology or from that of value. The present study has been concerned with aesthetics as a branch of the theory of value. It claims the merit of defining the aesthetic so broadly and dealing with it so comprehensively that its definitions are applicable also to the epistemological side of aesthetics. The fundamental conceptions have been developed, keeping in view always the broadest aspect of the philosophical science. At the same time, the satisfactory and adequate treatment of the problem of aesthetics considered as a branch of the theory of value has not been sacrificed. Aesthetics is based on a study of perceptual intuition. The aesthetic is the perceptual. Even if the interest in perceptual data is predominantly intellectual so that the perception is a perception of fact and no aesthetic value is apprehended, yet it remains true that the aesthetic element is always present. The lack of value indicates merely that the aesthetic attitude is not taken—that there is no pleasure resulting from the apprehension of the data for their own sake. It does not deny the apprehension of the data,

7.

The aesthetic element is fundamental to all experience. It is possible not only that all moral value may be dependent upon aesthetic value, but that all intellectual proof rests ultimately upon an aesthetic basis. The pragmatic view, when expressed as William James expressed it in his essay "The Sentiment of Rationality," [5] holds that rationality itself rests on a feeling of satisfaction in the apprehension of the data of experience. If we all want to make our soldiers march in a row, it is not only because they may be more efficient thus—they may not—but because we like to see rows. The ideals of system and order in scientific method are not wholly practical and useful. The demand that a logical or mathematical system be "simple" and "neat" in its delineation is an aesthetic demand. Croce says that the logical "principle of contradiction itself is at bottom nothing but the aesthetic principle of coherence." [6]

Even such a thinker as F. H. Bradley, in his essay "On Our Knowledge of Immediate Experience," [7] expresses a view that all which is known is dependent in the final analysis upon satisfaction or unrest in the immediate experience of the perceived object when perceived in relation to a "felt group." "Immediate experience is a positive non-relational non-objective whole of feeling." With the exception that the word "feeling" is

---

[5] In *The Will to Believe and Other Essays*, New York, 1897.
[6] B. Croce, *Aesthetic*, London, 1922, p. 44.
[7] In *Essays on Truth and Reality*, Oxford, 1914.

used in a vague sense, Bradley's treatment of immediate experience is a good characterization of the aesthetic experience. This is true despite the fact that at the end of the essay, in a footnote, he says that it is not. He says that he is aware of the claims of the aesthetic experience. He is thinking, however, of the aesthetic experience in the way in which it is usually defined: the experience of "beauty," a high degree of positive aesthetic value. If aesthetics be defined in an adequate manner, what he says is a characterization of the aesthetic.

Education cannot well dispense with the aesthetic. It has been pointed out that the use of charts, graphs, and diagrams is an appeal to the aesthetic sensibility.[8] If there is no apprehension of aesthetic value in the perception of these objects, it is because the aesthetic attitude is not taken toward them. Their usefulness, however, depends upon perceptual grasp. Education, to be adequate, must develop acute observation, and a training in art and appreciation can do this as nothing else can. Appreciation is based upon acute discernment of the perceptual aspects of an object. Hence, a training in appreciation is a training in observation and discrimination.

If education is the development of the natural powers of the individual, then aesthetic education should be given a major emphasis in contrast to the neglect which it suffers in many schools at present. The powers of perception must be developed and the pleasures that can be found in perception must be nurtured. Although they do not often show much appreciation of "beauty," most children show more spontaneous delight in

---

[8] See above, Chapter IV, Section 2.

perception than do many adults. Education should stimulate rather than suppress this tendency. It is the only foundation for genuine appreciation of aesthetic value, even in its most complex developments. Out of this delight is developed a complex and advanced standard of taste; and a developed standard of taste is of prime importance in a full and rich life. Aesthetic value is found when one takes pleasure in perception, and as perception is the background for all experience, humans might well take advantage of it as a source of pleasure. Aesthetic value is all-pervasive, and he is not wholly human who is not sensitive to it.

APPENDICES

APPENDIX A

Metaphysics and Aesthetics

1.

In the early history of aesthetics, the details of aesthetic theory were determined to a large extent by metaphysical considerations. For example, Plato, although he admitted the inspiration of the artist to be a heavenly madness, felt himself forced by metaphysical reasons to a position hostile to the free and genuine creation and appreciation of art. Aristotle emended Plato's aesthetic theory, but the emendations were dictated largely by the difference between his metaphysics and Plato's. By means of selection and emphasis, art displays the essence less encumbered by accidental characteristics, and so poetry may be truer than history.

In modern times, Baumgarten defines the study, for which he

invents the name "aesthetics," in order to fill in the outlines of the Leibnizian-Wolffian philosophy. Aesthetics, he says, is that which can be said in accordance with the prevailing metaphysics about sense knowledge and its perfection. Kant conceives the aesthetic judgment to be the final means of synthesis for the disparate realms of the pure and the practical reason, and for Kant, too, the metaphysical demands determined many of the details of his aesthetic theory. It is possible that this connection between his whole philosophical system and his aesthetics accounts for some of the parts of his theory not wholly satisfactory from the standpoint of aesthetics.[1]

Again, the character of Hegel's aesthetics is determined by his metaphysics. The identification of aesthetics with the philosophy of fine art is demanded not by a theoretic investigation of the aesthetic experience, but by metaphysical doctrines derived from other sources of inspiration. Probably the most influential figure in contemporary aesthetics is Croce; and although his aesthetics is not ostensibly an offshoot of a previously elaborated metaphysics, yet the heart of his doctrine, the identification of intuition and expression, is unintelligible except on the basis of an idealistic—almost a solipsistic—metaphysics.[2]

The endeavor of Appendix A, the present paper, will be to show that this historical tendency to make aesthetics dependent upon the solution or assumed solution of metaphysical problems is an incorrect method of procedure. It exactly reverses what would seem to be the correct application of the scientific method

---

[1] See Appendix B for an attempt to substantiate this point.

[2] See Appendix C for a further discussion of Croce.

both to the problems of aesthetics and to the problems of metaphysics. The thesis would apply to all other philosophical sciences as well as to aesthetics, but the present Appendix is concerned primarily with aesthetics.

2.

The scientific method is the unique contribution of European thought to history, and it has played a large part in both the material and the intellectual achievement of the past 2,500 years. A science, in this occidental sense, is a systematic and orderly body of knowledge, and the scientific method is the method of searching after knowledge in a systematic and an orderly way. *System* means that each part is consistent with all others, and all go together to form a coherent whole. Each has its place in the whole, and if the system is to be complete, there must be no indicated places left vacant. *Order* means that first things come first and middle things come in the middle and last things come last.[3] In an ordered series, there is some definite relation of precedence or succession between every two terms, and this relation is not reversible. Some rule may be found according to which the later terms may be derived from or constructed from the earlier. The most simple order type is that of the series of natural numbers. In this, all the numbers are obtained by the operation of adding one, and so are arranged in the order of magnitude. The first things, the smaller num-

---

[3] Although there are other types of order, the one referred to above is the type exemplified in the process of gaining knowledge.

bers, come first; the larger ones come in the middle; and the largest, if there were any, would come last.

In the field of knowledge known as natural science, it has been established by a long period of trial and error that the most fruitful method is, first, the careful observation of natural phenomena, and if possible, experimentation with them; then analysis and generalization, the formation of hypotheses, deduction, and verification. This is the correct application of the scientific method to the understanding of nature, because the first things are the things to be explained. These are the natural phenomena, and must be carefully observed under controlled conditions, if possible, to ensure completeness and correctness of observation. In Platonic language, the task of natural science is to "save the appearances"; hence the first step is to ascertain as accurately as possible what the appearances are. The next step is, through analysis and abstraction, to generalize on the basis of these observations, and thus to build up a theoretic explanation to connect and render coherent the mass of observed evidence. The formation of theory is constantly accompanied by verification from new observation and experiment; and by this means, the theoretic principles, at first only tentative and fragmentary, are elaborated into more and more complex structures, until finally, through deduction and testing, they are made more and more comprehensive and inclusive.

The process of acquiring theoretic knowledge in general is the process of building up more and more elaborate conceptual structures, and of endeavoring to reach principles of greatest generality and inclusiveness. All theory takes its rise from some element in experience. Logical form is abstracted from practical experience; it is the substance of all theory, and as the generality of logical form is increased, theoretic knowledge is attained. Analysis, abstraction, and generalization are the tools of this attainment, and the progressive interpretation and application of generalized logical form accompanies every step of the process.[4] In general, it may be said that in any kind of knowledge, the first things are the more simple elements of experience that enter into complex combinations and are the bases of simple generalizations. The scientific method would demand that in any investigation these first things should come first. The next things are the generalizations of narrow scope and the theories of less inclusiveness which are built upon these first things. The last things are those built on both the first and the middle: the principles of greatest generality and inclusiveness.

The nature of theoretic knowledge is that it is made up of precise and accurate generalizations of wide scope, and the scientific method is the crystallization of the best manner of attaining such generalizations. The scientific method of gaining knowledge, wherever applied, is the method of orderly progression in the investigation and solution of problems by working up from the more simple to the more complex, from the less general to the more general, from the less inclusive to the more inclusive; keeping an eye always on the possibility (even when it seems remote) of the co-ordination and coherence of such solutions into a systematic structure.

---

[4] I have endeavored to give a more detailed explanation of the relation of analysis, abstraction, and generalization to logical form in the first part of a paper "The Meaning of the Notation of Mathematics and Logic" in the *Monist*, Vol. XLI, No. 4, p. 594 (Oct. 1931).

3.

No one will doubt that metaphysical questions are the most general and inclusive that can be asked. Metaphysics is the attempt to find ultimate reality. It seeks principles for explaining and understanding all experience—any and every kind of experience. If this is the case, the formulation of precise and accurate metaphysical doctrines should be the summit and goal of all knowledge: not its point of departure.

Metaphysics is concerned with all experience. Natural science is concerned with that limited portion of experience called natural phenomena. The field of metaphysics is inclusive of the field of natural science; hence its theories are more general, and should be built upon as adequate a knowledge of natural science as possible. I do not say that metaphysical questions must be postponed until all the questions of natural science have been answered. I do wish to maintain two propositions: first, that metaphysical doctrines will be tentative and inadequate to the same or greater degree as are the theories of natural science. This is because metaphysical doctrines must be inclusive of the knowledge that can be ascertained by natural science. Second, that metaphysics can never dictate, even to the slightest degree, to natural science the solution of any of its problems. This is because the scientific method demands that the generalizations of natural science be based on the observation of natural phenomena. As metaphysical theory does not dictate the character of natural phenomena, it cannot dictate the principles of natural science.

I am aware that both the heliocentric theory and the atomic theory were suggested to natural science by metaphysics. I do not say that metaphysics cannot make suggestions; I say that it cannot dictate solutions. It is commonly held by that school of natural scientists which understands neither the aims nor the methods of philosophy that the method of natural science is not speculative. Nevertheless, it is speculative in a very important way. The formation of hypotheses is always speculative, as is, in fact, the enunciation of all theoretic principles. Metaphysics attempts to see all partial views in relation to a synoptic view, and, in its speculation concerning the relation between the phenomena of natural science and other kinds of reality, it may sometimes suggest hypotheses and theories that prove fruitful. Whether or not they prove fruitful cannot be determined by speculation alone, however. Verification of hypotheses in natural science depends upon the observation of empirical data.

The method of metaphysics is more highly speculative than is that of natural science, because metaphysics is interested in more than the experience of natural phenomena. Natural phenomena are those things that are known through ordinary sense perception. Things which are not known through ordinary sense perception may be approached only by reason, and it is this approach that we call speculative. For example, a word, as a physical sound, is an object of sense perception, but the word has a meaning, and this is not an object of sense perception. Epistemology investigates the problems of meaning (among other related problems); hence is not a natural science, and its method is more speculative than is that of natural science. The experience of the meanings of symbols, however, is a limited portion of our whole experience. As its field is delimited, epistemology is less general and less inclusive than is metaphysics, and because it is closer to the simple sources of one portion of experience, its approach to its problems is less speculative.

4.

Aesthetics is the study of the problems that center in the experience of a certain kind of value. A value is never an object of ordinary sense perception. The object which has the value may be. That is, I can see and touch a dollar bill, but I cannot see and touch the economic value residing in it. In a similar way, I can see a sunset or hear a symphony, but I cannot see or hear the aesthetic values residing in them. It is true that we often use language as if we could: we say that we see or hear the beauty. This is an elliptical expression. We see or hear the object which, when it comes into a certain relation to a sensibility, is beautiful. The beauty is an aesthetic value; and the investigation of this kind of value, the philosophic science of aesthetics, is speculative. It is less speculative than is metaphysics, because the object of its investigation is more particular and closer to the sources of our ordinary experience. Aesthetics deals with a delimited field, and therefore its principles are less general and less inclusive than metaphysical principles. Thus the relation between metaphysics and aesthetics is the same, and for the same general reasons, as was the case with natural science. First, metaphysical doctrines will be tentative and inadequate to the same or greater degree as are the doctrines of aesthetics. And second, metaphysics can never dictate, even to the slightest degree, the solution of aesthetic problems.

If the first statement is true, it is evident that no aesthetic doctrine can be dependent for certainty or intelligibility upon any metaphysical theory. No certainty could be derived from appeal to that which is necessarily of as little or less certainty than the doctrine to be guaranteed. And no intelligibility will be lent by an appeal to a theory which is at least as inadequate as the doctrine to be rendered intelligible. Ordinarily, intelligibility is obtained by subsuming whatever is to be explained under principles that are more general; but this is a real and not a specious intelligibility only when the general principles are themselves wholly intelligible. There is no vagueness or indefiniteness in generality unless there is some uncertainty about the particulars included under the generality or about the way in which they are related to the generality. The generalizations of metaphysics can be wholly intelligible only when the particulars of experience are clearly ascertained and when the relations between the partial generalizations of the separate sciences (which are built upon these particulars) and the wider generalizations of metaphysics are clearly apprehended. Now part of the field of metaphysics is given in aesthetics: those particulars treated in aesthetic theory and the theory as well. These, then, must be ascertained and substantiated before the generalizations of metaphysics are wholly intelligible. It must be aesthetics which contributes to the certainty and intelligibility of metaphysics, not the reverse; that is, if the scientific method is to govern our thinking.

If the second statement is true (that metaphysics can never dictate the solution of aesthetic problems), metaphysics may make suggestions and offer hypotheses to aesthetics, but cannot establish them. In fact, it would be of the greatest benefit to aesthetics if our metaphysical invention were more adequate so that more fruitful suggestions could be expected. These suggestions can be substantiated, however, only by their adequacy in covering and explaining any and all of the experience relevant to aesthetics. For example, if Croce is an idealist, he may suggest that intuition and expression are identical; and this may be a very fruitful suggestion. Whether or not it is must be determined without recourse to idealism or reliance upon it, for metaphysics has offered merely an hypothesis; it has not furnished evidences for proofs. Aesthetics must verify its hypotheses independently of metaphysics. Otherwise it abjures the scientific method. In so far as one's metaphysics would dictate that art is an imitation of an imitation, then so much the worse for the metaphysics.[5] And in so far as any metaphysics would indicate that the beauty of art is necessarily higher and greater than natural beauty, again, so much the worse for the metaphysics.

---

[5] I am not suggesting that Plato's metaphysics really demands this view.

5.

The position of this paper must not be construed to be anti-metaphysical. Metaphysics is the acme of all theoretic knowledge. It is adequate, however, only to the degree that it successfully assimilates all science—all fragmentary knowledge wherever it may be gained. The separate sciences may never be complete, and so it may be that complete metaphysical knowledge is impossible; but a partial metaphysics, in the sense of an attempt systematically and coherently to render intelligible all experience, is not impossible; and in the pursuit of this goal valuable suggestions to science may be made. A metaphysics following the scientific method cannot be rationalistic either in the sense of the seventeenth and eighteenth centuries (that metaphysics can be deduced from self-evident principles) or in the sense of Hegelian idealism (that metaphysics is attained by a dialectic process).

A metaphysical doctrine is an attempt systematically to interpret the whole of experience.[6] It arises from reflection upon experience; hence, there must be a large admixture of empiricism in any adequate metaphysics. This should not be the dogmatic empiricism of eighteenth-century England, which assumed that experience comes to the mind ready made. Metaphysics must be empirical in its beginnings, but it advances beyond these beginnings by means of reason. There is a "body

---

[6] Unless to speak of "the whole of experience" involves a fallacy of the mixture of types.

of presentedness" that is interpreted in any metaphysical system and must be explained and assimilated by it. This "body of presentedness" has been subjected to various kinds of interpretations and explanations in the history of human thought. The interpretation is rational. The "presentedness" is empirical, and an adequate metaphysics can never forget it. It is the starting point, and gives the evidence necessary to verify hypotheses. The interpretation must be an interpretation of the "body of presentedness." Again to use Platonic language, metaphysics as well as natural science must "save the appearances." The application of the scientific method to metaphysics demands that the study start with its starting point, that it formulate theoretic principles of explanation, and that these principles be verified again by experience.

One of the "appearances" which must be "saved" by any metaphysical theory is the aesthetic experience. No matter what one's metaphysical tenets are, there is the aesthetic experience to be dealt with philosophically. If experience in general is subject to interpretation from the standpoint of different metaphysical systems, then there ought to be found a certain number of theoretic principles underlying the aesthetic experience, and these principles themselves would be open to interpretation from the standpoint of any coherent metaphysical system. As long as no system of metaphysics seems to be completely substantiated, it would appear that the ideal of the philosophic science of aesthetics would be to elaborate a theoretic system subject to idealistic interpretations, to realistic interpretations, and others.

The scientific method demands that aesthetics be empirical

in the same sense as explained above for metaphysics. Aesthetics must start with its starting point, and that is the raw material of the aesthetic experience as roughly and preanalytically apprehended. The method of aesthetics must be autonomous, though not to the extent of forgetting the ideal of the systematic connection of all knowledge that is demanded by the scientific method. It is true, of course, that metaphysical questions can be asked about things aesthetic as they can be asked about anything. This does not mean that the solution of the systematic problems of aesthetics must wait upon the solution of ultimate metaphysical problems, or that they are bound up with any particular theory of metaphysics. It means that in the last analysis nothing is absolutely intelligible until all is interconnected through generalizations which serve to exhibit the relationships between all experience. The world has recently seen how close are the fundamental problems of physics and metaphysics, but even here, physics has led to metaphysics in the end. Physics is no more under the tutelage of metaphysics today than it was in the first flush of victory of the scientific revolution or in the great disdain of the nineteenth century. Nor can aesthetics be under the tutelage of metaphysics as long as the scientific method is professed. It is possible that we shall not perfectly know all there is to be known about aesthetics until we perfectly know all there is to know about everything. We shall not know much that is precise and accurate about everything, however, until we know a great deal that is fragmentary and tentative about each of the philosophic sciences. Precise metaphysical knowledge lies beyond the philosophic sciences.

It is true that the scientific method assumes some sort of a "principle of simplicity," but a metaphysical "founding" of this principle is in no way necessary in order to use it. In fact, the scientific method must be developed and used before any metaphysical substantiation of it would be more than mythology. One of the most profound things about Plato's philosophy is that it is an attempt metaphysically to justify the scientific method, but there is much mythology in Plato because the scientific method was then in its infancy, and his understanding of it was necessarily incomplete. If a metaphysical justification of the scientific method could be proposed, it would be of inestimable value. This is an outlook for metaphysics—not a record of accomplishment. What the scientific method is must first be ascertained before it can be metaphysically justified. It must be ascertained *in concreto*. Perhaps it has only a pragmatic justification. Perhaps it has no justification whatever except theoretic curiosity. But here too the "appearances" must be ascertained before they can be "saved." In so far as this paper has appealed to the scientific method, it has appealed to it merely as a methodological assumption.

An adequate metaphysics must be built up from the investigation of all experience. If it is formulated from the standpoint of other kinds of experience and then is applied to the aesthetic experience—that is, if the aesthetic experience is explained by an application of a metaphysical theory derived elsewhere—then it is not an adequate metaphysics, and the aesthetics cannot be an adequate aesthetics. An adequate aesthetics must always stay close to its sources in the actual aesthetic experience.

APPENDIX B

Kant's Theory of Aesthetics [1]

1.

In spite of the rapid growth and development of the theory of aesthetics in recent years, Kant's *Critique of Judgment* remains one of the most significant single contributions that has ever been made to aesthetic theory. This fact is often lost to sight because this work is usually regarded as only a part of his complete system of thought; but it has been of utmost importance in the history of aesthetics, and the germs even of some of the more recent developments in aesthetics can be found in it. For example, the central theses both of Santayana's doctrine and of Croce's are clearly stated in the *Critique of Judgment*. The theory of aesthetics elaborated in the preceding chapters owes much to the theoretic insights of Kant.

---

[1] Reprinted, by permission of the editors, from the *Philosophical Review*, Vol. XL, No. 6, Nov., 1931, with minor alterations.

Yet many puzzling questions arise from a study of Kant's theory of aesthetics. Why is it necessary for him to state his doctrine in paradoxes? Why did he change the meaning of the term *aesthetic* from that given in the *Critique of Pure Reason?* There Kant had used the word to mean "concerned with perception" (*Anschauung*—perceptual intuition). He noted that it was sometimes used concerning questions of taste, but he thought it advisable to drop that use for one nearer the etymology.[2] In the *Critique of Judgment,* however, he used *aesthetic* in the way that he had earlier thought inadvisable: his aesthetics here is an investigation of the judgment of taste. The ground of the judgment of taste is subjectively determined, and Kant consistently used the word aesthetic to mean subjective: referred to the subject and its feeling of pleasure and pain.

It is not necessary on Kant's own basis for him to change the meaning of the word aesthetic from *perceptual* to *subjective.* The earlier meaning is still fundamental in the *Critique of Judgment,* and the present appendix will endeavor to show that the change is due to a fundamental confusion between value and evaluation. This confusion results from Kant's interest in aesthetics as a means of effecting a synthesis between his other two Critiques.

2.

The first two Critiques had revealed realms between which "an immeasurable gulf is fixed"; and yet there must be some

---

[2] *Critique of Pure Reason,* Muller's translation, Second Edition, p. 17.

ground of unity or of synthesis of the two.[3] Kant attempted to supply this synthesis in the *Critique of Judgment*. The special investigation of the *Critique of Pure Reason* is the concepts of the understanding, and it reveals the realm of nature. That of the *Critique of Practical Reason* is the ideas of reason, and it reveals the realm of freedom. Judgment is a mediating link between the understanding and the reason, and if *a priori* principles of judgment can be found, these will afford the ground of the needed synthesis; the realms of nature and of freedom can be exhibited in harmony with each other. The critical investigation that is to disclose the *a priori* principles in judgment, and to discover whether they are objective or subjective, constitutive or regulative, is best served by the consideration of "those judgments that we call aesthetical"; that is, the judgment of taste.[4]

The importance of Kant's theory of aesthetics lies in the fact that it lays the foundations for a complete and adequate demarcation of the aesthetic experience from the intellectual by showing that the aesthetic is what pleases without a concept (or the intervention of a mediating idea);[5] and from the moral, by showing that the aesthetic is what pleases without desire.[6] Kant also shows that the aesthetic experience always involves the apprehension of form, and form is the unity in a manifold.[7]

---

[3] Introduction to the *Critique of Judgment,* Bernard's translation, p. 13. All the page references in Appendix B not otherwise assigned are to the *Critique of Judgment,* Bernard's Translation, Second Edition, London, 1914. Although I sometimes depart from Bernard, comparison with the German can readily be made from the page references to Bernard.

[4] See pp. 2, 3, and 4 of the Preface.

[5] P. 67.

[6] P. 55.

[7] Pp. 73–76.

The apprehension of form is immediately pleasing, but the pleasure is regarded not as a merely subjective state, but as if it were a part of the object.[8] It is true that he holds the apprehension of beauty to be a judgment, but he is thoroughly aware that it is not intellectual: it is not a logical judgment.[9] Yet, because of his method of approach to aesthetics, after intellectual considerations have been removed, they are introduced again by the back door.

This fact calls for a thorough investigation and criticism of Kant's method. In the first place, he divides all the faculties of the mind into three groups: faculties of knowledge (or cognition, *Erkenntnisvermögen*), faculties of desire, and faculties of feeling. Then he subdivides the faculties of knowledge into three parts: understanding, reason, and judgment. Each of these faculties of knowledge gives knowledge of one of the main groups: the understanding gives knowledge of knowledge, the reason gives knowledge of desire, and the reflective judgment, when aesthetical, gives knowledge concerning the feeling of pleasure and pain.[10]

Understanding, reason and judgment are co-ordinate faculties of cognition. The investigation of these three faculties gives rise to three Critiques, and as the faculties are co-ordinate, the Critiques proceed according to parallel methods. The fundamental problem of each is to find the *a priori* element which

---

[8] Pp. 33, 56.

[9] Kant continually insists on this. Among various passages, see especially pp. 80 and 157, and 158.

[10] Pp. 15–17 and 42. There may well be grave doubt that this division is anything but a schematical device (despite the footnote of p. 42), and that it is even consistent with other Kantian analyses. But this criticism will not be pursued in the present paper.

is involved in the use of the faculty it is investigating. According to Kant there is an *a priori* element in every kind of knowledge. This is what makes the synthesis of knowledge possible. Understanding, reason, and judgment all are cognitive faculties, and the exercise of each must involve *a priori* principles. Consequently, the Critiques that disclose the *a priori* principles should, in each case, proceed in the same manner. This parallelism of method extends throughout the general plan of each Critique.

3.

This is not a good method of procedure. It is based upon a faculty psychology which assumes that the three Critiques are investigations of parallel subject matter. They are not. Intellectual activities are different from valuing activities: cognition is not valuing, nor is valuing cognition. Both of the later Critiques are investigations of values. One might expect to find a degree of similarity of method in two theories of value, but to treat of values by a method parallel to that used for the treatment of knowledge is to invite confusion.

Kant's method causes the intrusion of intellectualism into his theory, as it would into any theory of aesthetics. For Kant, the apprehension of beauty is a result of the exercise of judgment. Judgment is, for him, a cognitive faculty; that is, it is intellectual. Judgment is the subsumption of a particular under a universal.[11] Of course, this is intellectual, because

---

[11] P. 17.

it involves activities of the understanding. Although the apprehension of beauty is a judgment for Kant, he is aware of the fact that it is not intellectual; hence he has recourse to the "reflective judgment," or the subsumption of a particular which is given under a universal which is not given (that is, of which we are not aware when we are making the judgment).[12] He holds that no aesthetically significant representation (*Vorstellung*) can be produced without the co-operation of the understanding.[13] The form of an object of perception (*Anschauung*) cannot be apprehended without the reflective judgment.[14] The cognition involved in this judgment, however, is *cognition in general*. As the understanding is not determined by a definite concept, it is in *free play*. The harmonious union of the imagination with the understanding in free

---

[12] P. 18. The reflective judgment may be a chimera. No direct evidence is given for it, and it is assumed or "presupposed" to account for the awareness of a particular (for which no universal is given) as pleasant. Kant holds that the particular must be thought in the unity of a "thoroughly connected experience" to account for the pleasure taken in its apprehension. See p. 24. It is difficult to interpret Kant upon the point: can there be any awareness of particulars outside of a thoroughly connected experience? This passage from the *Critique of Pure Reason* (p. 75, Muller's translation, Second Edition) indicates that there can: "It cannot be denied that phenomena [Kant would have said *Vorstellungen* instead of *Erscheinungen* in the language of the problem of the *Critique of Judgment*] may be given in intuition [*Anschauung*] without the functioning of the understanding." If there can be direct apprehension of perceptual data without the functioning of the understanding, and if the pleasantness of such apprehension can be accounted for directly, then the reflective judgment is an unnecessary assumption. If the reflective judgment is chimerical, there is no basis for anything *a priori* in the aesthetic experience, for the "deduction" of the *a priori* principle rests on the reflective judgment. See pp. 22–24, 152–153, 161–165. This, possibly, is only another indication that the aesthetic experience is not a kind of knowledge and is not essentially dependent upon the understanding.

[13] P. 64.

[14] P. 32.

play gives the representation which is the object of the judgment of taste.[15]

The universal concept which makes the reflective judgment possible appears in the judgment of taste (the appreciation of beauty) not as a concept, but only as a feeling.[16] In consequence of this, Kant says that the judgment of taste is not a cognitive judgment. He is led to believe that, although judgment usually is cognitive, the judgment of taste is not cognitive, because in it the concept appears only in a disguised form. At the same time that he says that the aesthetic judgment is not cognitive, he says that the use of the understanding, in harmony with the imagination, is involved in it.[17] For Kant, there is always a concept at the bottom of the experience of beauty, even if that concept is concealed.[18]

It is the business of the *Critique* to find this concept and display it, although it never enters into conscious experience. Kant finds it to be the concept of purposiveness, but there is no definite cognition of any purpose; there is only the form of purposiveness. This is what he means by purposiveness without purpose.[19] Although a beautiful object is always represented under the form of purposiveness, there is no specific purpose, but only the general purposiveness of its adaptability to the powers of perception. "Natural beauty brings with it a purposiveness in its form by which the object seems to be,

---

[15] P. 64.

[16] Pp. 65, 66. Kant in this passage uses *sensation* in the sense of feeling. See p. 49.

[17] Compare pp. 32, 64, 162, 169.

[18] P. 36.

[19] Pp. 68, 69.

as it were, pre-adapted to our judgment."[20]   The consciousness
of this "formal purposiveness in the play of the subject's cognitive powers, in a representation in which an object is given"
is a feeling—it is aesthetic pleasure.[21]   "This pleasure accompanies the ordinary apprehension of an object by the imagination, as faculty of intuition in relation with the understanding,
as faculty of concepts."[22]   To feel the pleasure is "merely
to perceive [*wahrzunehmen*] the accordance of the representation [*Vorstellung*] with the harmonious [*subjektive-zweck-
mässigen*] activity of both cognitive faculties [that is, imagination and understanding] in their freedom."[23]

4.

This, Kant's explanation of aesthetic pleasure, is intellectualistic. It involves activities of the understanding (though
disguised). A concept (though unrecognized) lies at the
bottom of it. Kant himself says that the pleasure is "referred
to concepts although indeterminate ones."[24]   The feeling of
pleasure is based on a judgment, though Kant insists that this
is a noncognitive judgment because the universal concept under
which the given particular (a representation, *Vorstellung*) is
subsumed is not given. Kant's whole method of approaching
the problems of aesthetics makes it impossible for him to keep
his theory free from intellectualism. Although it is clear that

---

[20] P. 103.
[21] P. 71.
[22] P. 169.
[23] Ibid.
[24] P. 101.

he is aware that the aesthetic experience is not intellectual, he describes it in intellectualistic terms.

The difficulty here is much deeper than a mere choice of terminology. There is a fundamental confusion lying at the base of his theory, due to his method of approach. It is the confusion between the apprehension of beauty and the judgment concerning this apprehension; that is, the confusion between value and evaluation. The distinction between the immediate apprehension of beauty and the knowledge of this apprehension is of utmost importance to a theory of aesthetics. Kant did not see the distinction, for he was interested in the aesthetic experience, not so much for the purpose of explaining it on its own account, as because he thought he saw in it the possibility of effecting a theoretical synthesis between the realms of nature and freedom. If, however, a theory of aesthetics is to be adequate *as aesthetics,* it must take its departure from the aesthetic experience, and not from some ulterior interest.

The aesthetic experience is an experience of value. Beauty is an aesthetic value. Value is immediately apprehended; not mediately as the result of intellectual processes (even though these be disguised). Hence, the apprehension of value is not intellectual or cognitive. It is possible, however, to have knowledge concerning this apprehension. One may know that he has an immediate experience of value. In fact, it may be that such knowledge is an invariable accompaniment of the immediate apprehension, but whether it is or not, it is something essentially different.[25] Such knowledge is embodied in judg-

---

[25] Any other view makes cognition and knowledge synonymous with consciousness, and therefore without special significance,

ments, and these judgments are, of course, cognitive and intellectual. They are *evaluations*. An evaluation is a judgment concerning values or valuings. All judgments are propositional in nature, and evaluations are propositional. Immediate experiences of value are not. They are direct.

No theory of any kind of value can avoid confusion unless the distinction between valuing and evaluating is clearly discerned. This cannot be emphasized too strongly. A value and an evaluation are not the same. Although aesthetics is concerned with evaluations as well as with values, it is concerned with them only because they are about values. If values and evaluations are not carefully distinguished, cognition is inextricably confused with immediate apprehension, because evaluations are cognitive. Any theory of value which holds that cognition is in some measure fundamental to direct apprehension should point out the exact degree to which it is fundamental. The attempt to do this leads to paradoxes. Kant's paradoxes already have been indicated in this paper, and explicit attention will be called to them later.

The individual apprehends values, and he also makes evaluations. The most compelling cause for making evaluations is the necessity of comparing values, and all comparison involves judgment. Comparison is propositional in nature: it is a relation between terms. Some values are more valuable than others, and the judgment that one is more valuable than another involves the recognition, explicit or implicit, of a factor which causes the difference. In the foregoing chapters, this was called the *evaluating factor*. It affords the measure of intensity of value. The complete definition of any particular kind of value must include its evaluating factor, but this accounts only for the comparison of different degrees of value, and not for the fundamental difference between one kind of value and another (for example, the difference between aesthetic and moral value).

The evaluating factor for aesthetic value is the feeling of pleasure. Pleasure, when it is felt while the subject is in the aesthetic attitude, is the measure of the intensity of the aesthetic value that is being apprehended. The more pleasure in the aesthetic attitude, the greater the degree of value. The degree of pleasure affords the means of comparison of aesthetic values. As Kant does not distinguish between the apprehension of aesthetic value and the comparison of different degrees of value, he makes the evaluating factor fundamental in his definition of the word *aesthetic*.

Kant's uses of the word *aesthetic* have already been noted in this paper. In the *Critique of Judgment,* he defines the word to mean "subjectively, not objectively, determined." He holds that it is subjectively determined because it is determined by the feeling of pleasure and pain.[26] In this way the evaluating factor becomes the predominant part of what he holds to be the fundamental meaning of the word *aesthetic*. It is impossible that the word be adequately defined or used in this way, because before an evaluating factor can be determined for aesthetic value, this kind of value must be differentiated from other kinds: that is, the fundamental meaning of the word *aesthetic* to which this evaluating factor is to be applied must be determined.

------

[26] P. 46.

5.

It is not necessary on Kant's own basis for him to define *aesthetic* as *subjective*. In the *Critique of Pure Reason*, he had used the word to mean *perceptual* (perceptual intuition, *Anschauung*), and even in the *Critique of Judgment* this meaning is still fundamental despite his consistency in intending always to mean *subjective*. There are numerous passages which bear out this interpretation. That which is subjective and concerned with feeling is aesthetic only in case it is also concerned with perception (*Anschauung*), for on page 133, Kant says that the absolutely good may be "subjectively judged according to the feeling that it inspires," and yet it is not aesthetic. In drawing the distinction between the aesthetical ideas and the rational ideas in Section 49, he constantly refers the aesthetic to perception (*Anschauung*). He does this also in Remark I to the Solution of the Antinomy of Taste (Section 57). On page 47 he says that whether or not a thing is beautiful depends on "how we judge it by mere observation (perception or reflection)." [27] On page 110 he says that the aesthetic estimation of magnitude "must consist in this, that we can immediately apprehend it in perception [*Anschauung*]." In a footnote on page 90, he explains that certain instruments are not beautiful because "there is not immediate

---

[27] *Anschauung oder Reflexion.* By "Reflection," Kant refers to the reflective judgment, which, as pointed out above, is only his way of accounting for the pleasantness of the immediate apprehension of a particular for which no universal is given.

pleasure in the perception [*Anschauung*] of them." All knowledge "not contained in the immediate perception [*Anschauung*]" is declared, on page 138, to be irrelevant to the aesthetic judgment. On pages 82 and 83 he maintains that "the pleasure in beauty . . . is immediately bound up with the representation [*Vorstellung*] through which the object is given." And he declares, on page 159, that to judge an object beautiful "I must feel the pleasure immediately in the representation of the object." For Kant, the representation (*Vorstellung*) is given in the imagination, and the imagination is the faculty of intuition or perception.[28]

Many other illustrations could be adduced to show that perceptual intuition (including the reproductive imagination) is fundamental to what is aesthetic for Kant in the *Critique of Judgment*. The question is, why did he think it necessary to change the meaning of the word to *subjective*? No answer is possible, except that owing to his confusion between value and evaluation he considered it necessary to include the evaluating factor for aesthetic value within the fundamental definition of the word *aesthetic*. The fundamental use of the word included a reference to pleasure because he failed to note the place of pleasure in the experience of value. It is obvious, however, that the meaning of the word *aesthetic* must be established before the place of pleasure in the aesthetic experience can be determined.

It might be noted that the above interpretation of why Kant

---

[28] See pp. 96, 169, and 198. It must be emphasized throughout that I am using the word *perception* only in the sense of *perceptual intuition*. Perception of fact (*Wahrnehmung*) is clearly intellectual, and is a very different matter.

thought it necessary to change the meaning of the word *aesthetic* from *perceptual* to *subjective* is further borne out by the fact that he considered the aesthetic judgment to be the judgment of taste, and the judgment of taste is the judgment that an object is beautiful. But the meanings of the words *taste* and *beautiful* both have reference to the comparison of values, for taste commonly denotes preference, and beauty denotes only a comparatively high degree of value. Therefore the meanings of these words involve the evaluating factor. By Kant's method of approaching aesthetics, the problems of evaluation are inextricably confused with the problems of value.

In actual wording, Kant's theory of aesthetics often seems to be a series of paradoxes. Some of the most striking of these are: judgment which is not cognitive; [29] universal validity which is only subjective; [30] knowledge which is not intellectual; [31] purposiveness without purpose; [32] necessity which is not apodictic; [33] knowledge which is without concept; [34] and the imagination's free conformity to law. [35] There are many others, and these recur repeatedly. If these paradoxes are necessary in the exposition of Kant's system, there is some antecedent error or fundamental confusion. Many of them arise directly from the definition of *aesthetic* as *subjective*. Beauty is subjective to Kant, and yet he shows that in the explanation of the experience it must be treated as if it were objective. [36] It did not

[29] P. 45.
[30] P. 60.
[31] P. 66.
[32] P. 68.
[33] P. 91.
[34] P. 96.
[35] P. 96.
[36] See pp. 56 and 58.

take his followers long to find out that it was as much objective as subjective to him, despite all his protests.

The presentation in perceptual intuition is fundamental to what is aesthetic in the *Critique of Judgment,* but Kant did not explicitly recognize the fact because he was preoccupied by the problem of the synthesis of his other two Critiques. He gives as a description of the aesthetic "whatever we present in intuition [*Anschauung*] *according to the precept of the judgment.*" [37] This precept is the subjective purposiveness of the judgment of taste. It is this subjectiveness which affords the grounds of synthesis between the realms of nature and of freedom. The doctrine of the subjective purposiveness of the aesthetic judgment (the apprehension of aesthetic value) is extremely important to Kant's theory of aesthetics considered as a *synthesis of his other two Critiques,* but it has no importance in his theory considered as a specific theory of aesthetics. It has even a place there only because of the fundamental confusion between value and evaluation, which has caused *aesthetic* to be defined as subjective.

6.

When one approaches the study of aesthetics from the standpoint of value, and sees that its central conception is a certain kind of value, all these confusions and paradoxes fall away. Value is neither subjective nor objective; but it is just as truly

---

[37] P. 109. Italics mine.

both subjective and objective. This is because the division into subjective and objective is not exhaustive. Value has a relational status, emerging from a relation between subject and object; therefore it seems to partake of some subjective conditions and some objective conditions. No confusions or paradoxes need arise from this situation if it is clearly realized.

The most fundamental meaning of the word *aesthetic* must be found. It must be fundamental enough adequately to differentiate aesthetic value from other kinds of value. Neither the meaning *feeling* nor the meaning *subjective* will do this. The meaning *perceptual* (as it has been used in the text of the preceding chapters) is adequate. The word *aesthetic* cannot be taken to mean "concerned with feeling," because aesthetic feelings must be distinguished from other kinds of feeling. It cannot be taken to mean pleasure, because there are other kinds of pleasure. That feeling or pleasure which is aesthetic is that which accompanies the intuition of perceptual data. Pleasure is the evaluating factor for aesthetic value; hence it is essential to a complete definition of *aesthetic value,* but is not essential to the fundamental meaning of the word *aesthetic.* Furthermore, the recognition of pleasure as the evaluating factor lays the basis for a satisfactory distinction between positive and negative aesthetic values. Kant was never clear about the relation between beauty and ugliness, nor does his method of approaching the problems of aesthetics give him any basis for a solution.

Kant's doctrine, considered as a theory of aesthetics, is not wholly satisfactory. There are elements in it that are the result of profound theoretic insight into the conditions of the aesthetic experience, but there are also elements in it that are intrusions—elements which result from confusions and lead to paradoxes. The way to avoid the paradoxes is to analyze the doctrine and find the elements in it that lead to them. Then, by purging the system of these errors, a more satisfactory solution of the problems of aesthetics can be achieved. The paradoxes result from the intellectualistic elements in the theory, which, in turn, result from the confusion of immediate experiences of value with judgments about those experiences, that is, the confusion of valuing with evaluating. The *Critique of Judgment,* as a theory of aesthetics, is the investigation of a certain kind of value, and hence the method which would be fruitful of adequate results would be the method which approaches the problem from the standpoint of value, and not from the standpoint of a use of reason co-ordinate with the theoretical use and the practical use. By such a method, all the essentials of Kant's theory can be preserved, and the parts which lead to paradoxes can be eliminated.

APPENDIX C

Croce, Carritt, and Aesthetic Value

The *Aesthetic* of Benedetto Croce probably has been the most influential work written within the field of aesthetics in recent years.[1] Many other writers, both English and American, are indebted to his thought. Among these, the English philosopher E. F. Carritt, although he acknowledges that he has been greatly influenced by Croce, cannot follow all the details of his theory. Carritt's method of exposition is different from Croce's, and he makes specific departures from Croce's doctrine. There are certain respects in which the theory of aesthetics presented in the preceding chapters is like the doctrine of Croce's. The differences are perhaps more striking than the likenesses, for much that Croce would consider essential to his theory could not be fitted within the present study. Nevertheless, a survey of Croce's theory, Carritt's

---

[1] English translation by Ainslie, Second Edition, London, 1922.

adaptation of it, and my criticisms of some aspects of both will shed much light on the theory of aesthetics contained within the preceding chapters, for although I agree with Carritt's criticisms, I come to conclusions that are in some ways diametrically opposed to his.

1.

Croce's thought is very important in the history of aesthetics, because he shows so conclusively that the aesthetic experience is an autonomous activity of the spirit, neither dependent upon other modes of spiritual activity, nor to be subsumed under them. It is not intellectual, moral, or utilitarian.[2] Croce distinguishes the aesthetic from the intellectual adequately and forcefully by showing that the aesthetic depends upon intuition. Intuition is a kind of knowledge, but is clearly differentiated from logical or conceptual knowledge. Intuition is imagination: it gives knowledge of the individual, and is productive of images. "Intuition" and "vision" are synonymous.[3]

Croce then declares that intuition and expression are identical. The expression which is intuition, however, is a spiritual activity and must be carefully distinguished from what is or-

---

[2] This, perhaps, is presented more concisely in the *Breviary of Aesthetic* than in the *Aesthetic*. See the *Breviary*, pp. 436–447 and pp. 480–481. Croce's *Breviary of Aesthetic* (English translation by Ainslie) is printed in the Rice Institute *Book of the Opening*, Vol. II, pp. 430–517. All references to the *Breviary* in this Appendix are to these pages. The *Breviary* is also printed in the Rice Institute Pamphlets, Vol. II, No. 4, December, 1915. It is more easily available in England under the title *The Essence of Aesthetic*, London, 1921.

[3] See the *Breviary*, p. 436.

dinarily called expression: "expression in the naturalistic sense." [4] Expression in the naturalistic sense refers to an external sign, whereas true expression is always internal; it is an ideal fact. [5] What is called expression in everyday language is only a symptom of a spiritual state, whereas aesthetic expression *is* a spiritual state. Expression has "the very character of activity and spirituality"; it is a "spiritual synthesis." [6] It is necessary to understand this in order to understand the nature of intuition, for "the spirit only intuits in making, forming, expressing." [7]

This intuition or expression is the aesthetic or artistic fact. [8] Croce rarely uses the word "art" to denote the physical object often called the work of art (and so called in the preceding chapters). [9] He says that to call the external thing art "is simply a question of a linguistic usage, doubtless permissible, though perhaps not advisable." [10] For his own usage, he insists that the work of art (the aesthetic work) is always *internal*." [11] Croce denies that art is a physical fact. [12] Art is a spiritual activity. Art is expression. Nothing else than this intuitive vision is truly aesthetic. The physical object sometimes called the work of art is only an externalization of the artist's vision, and is produced by a "practical activity directed

---

[4] *Aesthetic,* p. 95.
[5] See the *Aesthetic,* pp. 8–9, 50, and 108.
[6] *Ibid.,* pp. 95 and 96.
[7] *Ibid.,* p. 8.
[8] *Ibid.,* p. 12.
[9] See above, Chapter IX, Sections 1–2.
[10] *Aesthetic,* p. 51.
[11] *Ibid.,* p. 51. Italics his.
[12] *Breviary,* p. 436.

to producing stimuli to aesthetic reproduction." [13] This activity of reproduction does not have any essential connection with aesthetic expression, though Croce does not deny that the artist may sometimes achieve the full depth of his vision while working with the external means of reproduction.[14]

All that is truly aesthetic, being internal, is subjective. Intuition is expression, art is expression, beauty is expression.[15] The aesthetic activity may have a physical or psychophysical side; but to the question of whether it *really* possesses this side or only seems to possess it, Croce gives an unqualified answer that it only seems to possess it.[16] Beautiful things and physical beauty are only elliptically so called.[17] "The beautiful is not a physical fact; it does not belong to things, but to the activity of man, to spiritual energy." [18] It is true that Croce asserts that the receiving of impressions precedes expression, but impressions are not aesthetic.[19]

Croce insists that intuition is not perception, but when he does so, he uses the term perception only in the sense of perception of fact. Perception is "the apprehension of something as *real*," [20] whereas "the distinction between reality and nonreality is extraneous, secondary to the true nature of intuition." [21] Croce's concept of intuition is, perhaps, not so very different from that of perceptual intuition elaborated in the

---

[13] *Aesthetic,* p. 111.
[14] *Ibid.,* p. 118.
[15] *Breviary,* p. 470.
[16] *Aesthetic,* p. 94.
[17] *Ibid.,* p. 98.
[18] *Ibid.,* p. 97. See also p. 109.
[19] *Ibid.,* pp. 15–16. See also pp. 96 ff.
[20] *Ibid.,* p. 3. Italics his.
[21] *Ibid.,* p. 3.

preceding chapters (with one important exception), for he says that "intuition gives us the world, the phenomenon," [22] and he denies that there can be any intellectual intuition.[23] The one important exception noted is that the perceptual intuition of the preceding chapters is not expression; but perhaps this disagreement with Croce does not record so much of a difference between the two concepts of intuition as it does between those of expression.

2.

E. F. Carritt, in the *Theory of Beauty*, says that he thinks "a greater amount of truth is contained in Croce's *Estetica* than in any other philosophy of beauty that I have read." [24] He cannot agree with Croce, however, in identifying intuition and expression. He maintains that this identification can be made only by assuming an idealistic metaphysics that is plainly subjective and possibly solipsistic.[25] Carritt is not willing to base his aesthetic theory on this metaphysical position, and he thinks Croce has not proved the identification.[26]

Despite his disagreement, Carritt thinks that Croce has correctly indicated the general region in which beauty and aesthetic value is to be found. Much of importance in Croce's work is independent of the identification.[27] Croce has put his finger

---

[22] *Ibid.*, p. 31. See also p. 60.
[23] *Ibid.*, p. 66.
[24] *The Theory of Beauty*, London, 1923, p. 281.
[25] *Ibid.*, pp. 196–204.
[26] *Ibid.*, p. 288.
[27] *Ibid.*, p. 204.

on the considerations necessary to the definition of the aesthetic experience, and has furnished the foundation for attaining an understanding of it; but he has gone too far in identifying intuition and expression. Carritt feels not only that this doctrine is based on an unproved metaphysical assumption, but that it really does not add anything to the value of Croce's insights. Hence, Carritt rejects the identification and finds the essence of the experience in expression alone.[28] Even here, however, he does not wholly agree with Croce, for he holds that not any and every kind of expression is aesthetic. Croce makes no distinctions. Carritt thinks that if one does not limit the kind of expression, he has to agree with Croce that aesthetic and linguistic are the same thing.[29] Carritt does not make this identification. He limits aesthetic expression to the expression of feeling or emotion (using the term *emotion* in a broad sense, not narrowly psychological).[30]

Carritt distinguishes expression from symptom in the same way as does Croce.[31] He does not use the term *art* as a synonym of the whole aesthetic experience, but this is largely a matter of terminology, for Carritt, not rejecting the external existence of the object of the aesthetic experience, finds it desirable to distinguish those objects that are the products of human artifice from those that are not, and thus he talks about the beauties of art and the beauties of nature.[32] As nature and

---

[28] *Ibid.*, pp. 296 ff.
[29] See the *Aesthetic*, Chapter XVIII, and the *Breviary*, p. 471.
[30] *The Theory of Beauty*, pp. 287–288. Croce himself says almost this in pp. 454–456 of the *Breviary*, but not in so emphatic a way.
[31] *The Theory of Beauty*, pp. 296 and 297.
[32] *Ibid.*, pp. 35–38.

works of art are not subjective to Carritt, it is not clear how beauty could be as completely subjective to him as to Croce; but all beauties are homogeneous because all are expression, and expression is subjective according to Carritt's definition. Hence, beauty is subjective. "It is not the written or spoken poem nor the perceived atmospheric conditions which must strictly be called beautiful, but only a particular way in which at a given moment any individual expresses himself in them." [33]

3.

I agree with Carritt in the admission of great value to Croce's work: the essence of the aesthetic experience is to be found in the region which Croce has pointed out. Furthermore, I agree that Croce has not substantiated the identity of intuition and expression without metaphysical bias. I would go even further and say that the doctrine is only the statement of a metaphysical position, and is not an aesthetic theory. I have given in detail in Appendix A my reasons for holding that the problems of aesthetics cannot be solved by recourse to metaphysical dogmas. Before Croce or anyone else has a right to base his aesthetic theory upon metaphysical doctrines, those doctrines must be established beyond the shadow of a doubt. I do not hold that Croce's doctrines are so established.

Although I agree with all of Carritt's criticisms of Croce, I disagree radically with his conclusions, nevertheless. Because Carritt cannot accept the doctrine of the identity of intuition

---

[33] *Ibid.*, p. 298.

and expression, he drops the concept of intuition and defines aesthetic value in terms of expression. The present volume, on the other hand, defines aesthetic value in terms of intuition.[34]

The question here is, how can that which is valuable in Croce's doctrine be conserved while his metaphysical hypotheses and that which is either obscure or inadequate for any reason are discarded? The present discussion asserts that the theoretic value of Croce's work for the study of aesthetics is all comprehended within the definition of aesthetic value in terms of perceptual intuition. The metaphysical identification of intuition with expression serves, within aesthetics, no purpose whatever.

The present discussion also asserts that Carritt's definition of beauty in terms of expression alone in no way betters Croce's theory. It does not clarify any obscurity which Croce's system does not; it uses language with violence; and it does not effectively escape the identification of intuition with expression, to which Carritt objects.

When I say that Croce and Carritt do violence to language, I mean that they define "expression" in a way that departs from the usual meaning of the term. Expression, in ordinary discourse, means the act of uttering, or that which is uttered. Expression may also mean the revelation of meaning or feeling. To reveal means to make plain, to divulge, or to communicate. Perhaps it is not essential to the definition that actual communication take place, but the form which makes communication

---

[34] It must be borne in mind constantly that the intuition of the present work is perceptual intuition only. Whether or not there is any other kind of intuition is not at issue. A decision on this point belongs to epistemology, not to aesthetics. If Croce supposes any other kind to be aesthetic, then that is another point where the present theory departs from him.

possible is essential to the ordinary meaning of the word. Expression is putting some mental content into the form that makes communication possible.

An expression, in the sense that it may communicate something from one person to another, is only a symptom in the terminology of Croce and Carritt.[35] One does not express anger by a scowl: this is only a symptom of anger. One can really express anger only by imagining (or intuiting, in the language of Croce) a suitable poem or picture or piece of music. It is this use of the term expression to which I refer as doing violence to language.

Carritt's doctrine is that the external revelation of a feeling is not expression. The expression of a feeling is the revelation of the nature of the feeling *to the person who is experiencing it.*[36] It is whatever gives "form and pressure" to "impulses and aversions in our practical nature which can only thus become the objects of contemplation."[37] It is "becoming aware, not indeed of the nature of things, but of our own inner nature and processes, which are conditioned by things and which were before obscure to us."[38] By "becoming aware" Carritt does not mean "knowing about," because that would be intellectual. Becoming aware means having an inner realization. Hence, this definition says, in effect, that expression is not *vaguely* feeling a feeling, but *definitely* feeling a feeling, so that it can become the object of (a nonintellectual) contemplation.

Garritt rejects Croce's identification of expression with intui-

---

[35] *Croce, Aesthetic,* p. 95. Carritt, *The Theory of Beauty,* pp. 296 and 297.
[36] *The Theory of Beauty,* p. 182.
[37] *Ibid.,* p. 279.
[38] *Ibid.,* p. 111.

tion, yet his definition of expression has much in common with Croce's definition of intuition. In the *Aesthetic,* Croce does not emphasize feeling, but in the *Breviary,* he defines intuition as "feeling become contemplation." [39] In the article entitled *Aesthetics* in the fourteenth edition of the *Encyclopaedia Britannica* he uses "contemplation of feeling," "lyrical intuition," and "pure intuition" in apposition to each other, and he defines intuition as the union of feeling and image. [40] Of course, Croce defines intuition and expression in the same way, for they are the same thing. Carritt does not accept the view that they are the same thing, yet defines expression in the same way as does Croce.

The way in which Carritt defines expression makes Croce's identification of the two plausible. In fact, it is not Croce's view of intuition that yields the identity, but his view of expression. It is impossible for Carritt to distinguish between expression and symptom except by means of the same doctrine of expression which leads Croce to make the identification. Carritt holds that expression is an inward realization. This is also what intuition is. Expression may be mediated by external and objective situations. So may intuition. Expression may, at other times, be due wholly to the activities of the imagination. So may intuition. If expression means what Carritt says it means, it is very much like intuition. But he cannot agree that they are the same. Why not? Of course, if expression means what it is usually taken to mean, it has not a great deal in common with intuition, but is an activity succeeding intuition. Carritt

---

[39] *Breviary,* p. 456.
[40] *Encyclopaedia Britannica,* Vol. 1, p. 264, first column.

seems to approach the subject always from the standpoint of the usual meaning of expression. This leads him to disagree with Croce in the identification. Then he proceeds to define expression in the manner that makes the identification possible.

In *The Theory of Beauty,* Carritt says that the best description of the experience of beauty "seems to be that in it we embody or express in sensible form our feelings; bring before our minds for contemplation what we had already somehow been or done." [41] It appears to me that the apposition "embody or express" appeals to the usual understanding of the meaning of expression, but certainly, the part of the quotation coming after the semicolon, which I take to be explaining what expression is, sounds very much like intuition. It sounds like intuition as Croce uses the term, and it could be called a kind of perceptual intuition as that is defined in the preceding chapters. It is a description of imagination, and imagination is a kind of intuition. [42]

4.

The upshot of the whole matter is that the way Croce defines expression does make expression and intuition identical. Hence, if Carritt accepts the definition, he cannot avoid the identification. The reasons for rejecting the identification seem impelling to me. I accept all those given by Carritt, and in addition say that the identification does violence to the ordinary

---

[41] *The Theory of Beauty,* p. 298.
[42] See above, Chapter III, Section 6.

use of language. There is nothing sacred in the ordinary use of language, but the purpose of philosophy is to attain clear understanding. A use of language out of the ordinary is necessary if the ordinary use is confused or the result of a confusion of fundamental categories. Even where necessary, it is regrettable, for it hampers the task of philosophy and makes it more difficult. Therefore, in so far as philosophy departs from the ordinary use of language without cause and necessity, such departure is pernicious.

The distinction between intuition and expression is not only valid, but is a proper one to introduce into the terminology of aesthetic theory. There is a difference between subject and object in experience. It is legitimate and necessary to record this in the conceptual scheme of philosophy. Aesthetics needs a concept for what I have called perceptual intuition. If the distinction between subject and object is to be reflected in the categorial scheme of aesthetics, we need another concept for the act of putting intuition into the form which makes communication possible. If there were no possible communication and nothing objective in experience, such a concept would be unnecessary, but objective conditions are actually used for the purpose of communication. Hence, we need this second concept which I would like to call "expression": it fits well with the usual use of language to do so. Expression is the act of putting any mental content into the form which makes communication possible.

I agree with Croce that it is not essential to expression that any actual communication take place. One may as completely express something to himself as to another. Often his intuition is not completely clear until he does so. This fact, however, does not make the intuition the same as the expression. The fact remains that the expression uses objective conditions in a way that intuition does not. The expression involves intellectual and practical considerations which, strictly, are beyond aesthetics. They are beyond aesthetics, but they are not irrelevant, for if one admits the possibility of communication of the aesthetic experience (that is, the possibility of constructing a physical object which will awaken an experience even remotely similar to the original experience), the conditions of the communication are relevant to aesthetics.

Croce, because of his subjective idealism, does not seem to recognize the need of the concept I have called "expression" in distinction from the one I have called "perceptual intuition." I hold that it is necessary regardless of the reality, metaphysically defined, of the objective conditions which make communication possible. The object may be either an activity of spirit, a projection of Absolute Mind, or an independently existing material thing, it matters no whit. Whatever the object really is, if it appears in our experience, philosophical analysis must take account of it. I take account of it by admitting a concept of expression which is different from intuition.

One of the reasons Croce gives for rejecting the separate concept of expression is that he holds the definitive nature of the intuition itself to have all the form necessary for communication. I think the fact that I can clearly recognize what I cannot reproduce is evidence that the form of intuition is not sufficient for communication. The problem of the use of technique indicates a difference between the form of intuition and the form necessary for communication. There are many kinds of form. Aesthetic form is the form of perceptual intuition. There is no necessary reference to communication or to the possibility of communication in this definition. The form of expression is more than the form of intuition, because it involves dealing with what appears to be an object in such a way as to make that object serve as a means of communication from my own consciousness to what I suppose is some other consciousness. Even though all this may be metaphysically unreal, the appearances are there; hence, it is necessary in aesthetics to distinguish between intuition and expression.

Croce's definition of expression serves no purpose except within his metaphysical doctrine. It has no value to aesthetics. I am fully aware that Croce would reject the distinction between aesthetics and metaphysics which I am assuming here.[43] What I mean by the distinction and why I hold it are given in Appendix A.

An adequate understanding of the aesthetic experience can be attained without the violence toward language which is to be found in Croce's and Carritt's definition of expression. The aesthetic experience is perceptual intuition, and thus all aesthetic value is founded on the activity of intuition.[44]

---

[43] See the preface to the *Aesthetic*. "Strictly speaking, there are no particular philosophic sciences."

[44] It would be a mistake to assume from the foregoing that the genesis of the theory embodied in the present volume lay in a study of Croce and Carritt. As a matter of fact, the point of departure for my own thought was Santayana's *Sense of Beauty*. I became aware of the relation between my own views and those of Croce and Carritt only after the theory of the present work was rather fully formulated.

INDEX

Index